THE REFLECTION GUIDE TO

BETTER
CONVERSATIONS

//

COACHING OURSELVES AND EACH OTHER
TO BE MORE CREDIBLE, CARING, AND CONNECTED

ISBN 978-1-5063-3883-5

The Reflection Guide to Better Conversations: Coaching Ourselves and Each Other to Be More Credible, Caring, and Connected

Jim Knight, Jennifer Ryschon Knight, Clinton Carlson

Published by Corwin, Thousand Oaks, California
Printed in the United States of America
Cover design by Clinton Carlson

Certified Chain of Custody
SUSTAINABLE Promoting Sustainable Forestry
FORESTRY www.sfiprogram.org
INITIATIVE SFI-01268

SFI label applies to text stock

TABLE OF CONTENTS

INTRODUCTION AND GETTING STARTED

We are living through a communication crisis.

Effective communication is an essential skill for a fulfilled life.

Communication is central to school improvement.

INTRODUCTION

////////////////////////

> "We have found that the single factor common to every successful change initiative is that relationships improve. If relationships improve, things get better. If they remain the same or get worse, ground is lost. Thus leaders must be consummate relationship builders with diverse people and groups—especially with people different than themselves."
> //////////////
> **MICHAEL FULLAN**
> *Leading in a Culture of Change*

Practicing effective communication is clearly one of the first and best things we can do as professionals to improve our relationships and school culture, which in turn will make it far more likely that every student in every class will be receiving the very best instruction every day. The book, *Better Conversations: Coaching Ourselves and Each Other To Be More Credible, Caring, and Connected*, has distilled what is generally recognized and known to be the best, immediately useful, and most effective ideas of good communication to date. However, knowing about the best ideas in communication is of little help if we don't have a practical plan in place to begin to translate these ideas into daily practice. This book will help you solidify in your mind the beliefs and habits of Better Conversations and then guide you as you begin to coach yourself individually or with a team toward mastery of these Better Conversation Habits.

Never before has it been so easy for us to coach ourselves on our communication skills. Anyone with a smartphone or tablet can push the red button, record a conversation (when their conversation partner is agreeable), and see how effectively they listen, build emotional connections, give positive feedback, and so forth. The little computer in our pocket helps us clearly see our current reality, set goals, and monitor our progress toward those goals. With a little effort, we can quickly, permanently, and dramatically improve our relationships with others.

We have found that we can start to have better conversations by following a three-step cycle for improvement: identify, learn, and improve. In the following pages, you'll be guided through how to use the Improvement Cycle and set goals to dramatically change your communication practice for the better.

This companion guide to Better Conversations is divided into two sections. First, you'll think about what you believe about communication and learn about the six Better Conversations Beliefs. In the second section of the book, you'll review the 10 Habits of Better Conversations and begin coaching yourself as you practice to gain mastery of these habits.

Let's begin by asking: Where are you now? Where do you want to be?

To begin the process of learning about how you communicate now and how you want to communicate, complete the Communication Profile included here to take stock of your communication skills. Consider sharing the one-column survey with your closest friends, colleagues, and family members and ask them to fill out the form anonymously. Keep these forms nearby as you work through the Better Conversations Habits. You may want to change your assessment of where you are as you move through this book.

Communication Profile

//

WHERE I AM RIGHT NOW		**WHERE I WANT TO BE**
UNTRUE · · · · · · · · · VERY TRUE 1 2 3 4 5 6 7 8 9 10	I listen effectively.	UNTRUE · · · · · · · · · VERY TRUE 1 2 3 4 5 6 7 8 9 10
UNTRUE · · · · · · · · · VERY TRUE 1 2 3 4 5 6 7 8 9 10	I build emotional connections.	UNTRUE · · · · · · · · · VERY TRUE 1 2 3 4 5 6 7 8 9 10
UNTRUE · · · · · · · · · VERY TRUE 1 2 3 4 5 6 7 8 9 10	I ask questions effectively.	UNTRUE · · · · · · · · · VERY TRUE 1 2 3 4 5 6 7 8 9 10
UNTRUE · · · · · · · · · VERY TRUE 1 2 3 4 5 6 7 8 9 10	People trust me.	UNTRUE · · · · · · · · · VERY TRUE 1 2 3 4 5 6 7 8 9 10
UNTRUE · · · · · · · · · VERY TRUE 1 2 3 4 5 6 7 8 9 10	I praise others effectively.	UNTRUE · · · · · · · · · VERY TRUE 1 2 3 4 5 6 7 8 9 10
UNTRUE · · · · · · · · · VERY TRUE 1 2 3 4 5 6 7 8 9 10	I control my emotions effectively.	UNTRUE · · · · · · · · · VERY TRUE 1 2 3 4 5 6 7 8 9 10
UNTRUE · · · · · · · · · VERY TRUE 1 2 3 4 5 6 7 8 9 10	I treat others as equals.	UNTRUE · · · · · · · · · VERY TRUE 1 2 3 4 5 6 7 8 9 10
UNTRUE · · · · · · · · · VERY TRUE 1 2 3 4 5 6 7 8 9 10	My conversations are usually good for me and my partner.	UNTRUE · · · · · · · · · VERY TRUE 1 2 3 4 5 6 7 8 9 10
UNTRUE · · · · · · · · · VERY TRUE 1 2 3 4 5 6 7 8 9 10	I frequently find common ground with other people.	UNTRUE · · · · · · · · · VERY TRUE 1 2 3 4 5 6 7 8 9 10
UNTRUE · · · · · · · · · VERY TRUE 1 2 3 4 5 6 7 8 9 10	I am fully present in all conversations.	UNTRUE · · · · · · · · · VERY TRUE 1 2 3 4 5 6 7 8 9 10
UNTRUE · · · · · · · · · VERY TRUE 1 2 3 4 5 6 7 8 9 10	I successfully redirect destructive conversations.	UNTRUE · · · · · · · · · VERY TRUE 1 2 3 4 5 6 7 8 9 10
UNTRUE · · · · · · · · · VERY TRUE 1 2 3 4 5 6 7 8 9 10	I collaborate effectively with others.	UNTRUE · · · · · · · · · VERY TRUE 1 2 3 4 5 6 7 8 9 10

Communication Profile

//

Please record your personal opinion of how true or untrue the following statements are with respect to the subject of this survey. Effective communication is an essential part of a successful, fulfilling life, and by giving your honest opinion, you can help the subject of this survey make important improvements.

UNTRUE ——— VERY TRUE	Statement
1 2 3 4 5 6 7 8 9 10	Listens effectively.
1 2 3 4 5 6 7 8 9 10	Builds emotional connections.
1 2 3 4 5 6 7 8 9 10	Asks questions effectively.
1 2 3 4 5 6 7 8 9 10	Is trusted by people.
1 2 3 4 5 6 7 8 9 10	Praises others effectively.
1 2 3 4 5 6 7 8 9 10	Controls emotions effectively.
1 2 3 4 5 6 7 8 9 10	Treats others as equals.
1 2 3 4 5 6 7 8 9 10	Engages in conversations that are usually good for everyone involved.
1 2 3 4 5 6 7 8 9 10	Frequently finds common ground with other people.
1 2 3 4 5 6 7 8 9 10	Is fully present in all conversations.
1 2 3 4 5 6 7 8 9 10	Successfully redirects destructive conversations.
1 2 3 4 5 6 7 8 9 10	Collaborates effectively with others.

Goals

///////////////

As you begin to consider the things you want to change and start thinking about setting goals that can help you get to where you want to be, you'll need to understand more about how to set effective goals.

We have found that effective goals have five characteristics. Each of the characteristics is described below.

PEERS GOALS
  » Powerful
  » Easy
  » Emotionally Compelling
  » Reachable
  » Specific and Measurable

POWERFUL
If we are going to work hard to achieve a goal, we need to be sure the goal we're striving to hit is worth the effort. A powerful goal is one that will dramatically improve our lives, the lives of the people with whom we interact, and have a long-term positive impact.

EASY
Powerful goals that are difficult or impossible to implement are not as helpful as powerful goals that are easy to implement. Difficult-to-implement goals, no matter how powerful, often end up on the scrap heap of unrealized good intentions. In *Influencer: The Power to Change Anything* (2008), Patterson and his colleagues explain why easy and powerful goals are so important, "When it comes to altering behavior, you need to help others answer only two questions. First: Is it worth it? And second, Can they do this thing? Consequently, when trying to change behaviors, these are the only two questions that matter."

EMOTIONALLY COMPELLING
In their book *Switch: How to Change Things When Change Is Hard* (2010), Heath and Heath suggest that effective goals need to be more than SMART; they need to compel people to action by moving them emotionally. According to the authors, effective goals "provide a destination postcard—a vivid picture from the near-term future that shows what could be possible" (p. 76).

REACHABLE

Achieving a goal builds confidence, efficacy, and hope. When I reach a goal, I'm more confident that I can reach other goals. However, not hitting a goal can have the opposite effect. Unachieved goals decrease my confidence, efficacy, and hope. Shane Lopez, a researcher at the University of Kansas and The Gallup Organization, has been described as the world's leading expert on hope. In *Making Hope Happen: Create the Future You Want for Yourself and Others* (2013), Lopez writes that hope requires three elements. First, hope requires a goal that sets out an idea of "where we want to go, what we want to accomplish, who we want to be" (p. 24). Second, to feel hope, we need agency, our "perceived ability to shape our lives day to day ... [our knowledge that] ... we can make things happen" (p. 25). Finally, hope requires pathways, "plans that carry us forward" (p. 25).

SPECIFIC AND MEASURABLE

Finally, a reachable goal also has to be one that people will know they have reached. That is, as SMART goals have shown for years, the goal has to be specific and measurable. For example, being a better listener is not an effective goal, but reducing interruptions to no more than one each 15 minutes is clear.

SHANE LOPEZ'S ELEMENTS OF HOPE: GOALS, AGENCY, PATHWAY

A goal that fosters hope is a goal that has a reasonable chance of being achieved because (a) we believe we can achieve it (agency) and (b) it includes a strategy or strategies that can help us achieve it (pathways).

Coaching Yourself to a Better Conversation

The second part of this book is where you will begin to learn and practice the Better Conversations Habits. At the end of each section, there are reflection forms to use as you watch your video and begin setting goals. You'll use the Looking Back forms to review previous conversations and clarify your current communication habits. Then, you'll use the Looking At forms to begin to gauge where you are now. Finally, you'll use the Looking Ahead forms to help you set specific goals for future conversations.

You can set a goal and begin to use the Improvement Cycle to coach yourself by video recording an important conversation (it could be a conversation at home, work, in the community, or somewhere else) and then watching the recording with the Communication Profile form nearby to focus your attention on various aspects of your interaction. Often, it is extremely easy to identify a goal after watching only a few minutes of video; at other times the form is essential to help us clarify where we want to improve.

No communication habit is guaranteed to work as described, and often habits need to be modified or rebooted to work for particular individuals. Sometimes by watching yourself on video and implementing a habit as described in the book, you can quickly meet your goal. At other times you need to modify or change your approach until you achieve what you set out to accomplish. Once a goal has been met, you can set another goal and keep having better and better conversations.

"Before you begin a thing, remind yourself that difficulties and delays quite impossible to foresee are ahead. If you could see them clearly, naturally you would do a great deal to get rid of them but you can't. You can only see one thing clearly and that is your goal. Form a mental vision of that and cling to it through thick and thin."
////////////////,
KATHLEEN NORRIS

Coaching

THE IMPROVEMENT CYCLE

/////////////////.

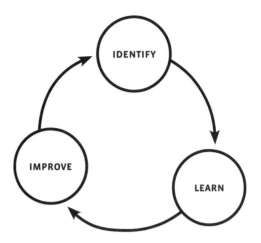

IDENTIFY (A)

Use a smartphone or tablet to record a conversation.

If you are going to try to get better you need to understand your current reality. Put another way, if you are going somewhere, you need to know where you are starting. The easiest way to get a clear picture of reality when it comes to understanding how you communicate is by recording yourself talking.

Start by video recording yourself communicating because if you are like most other people, you have a very poor understanding of what it looks like when you interact with others. In fact, just seeing yourself in conversation can be a huge catalyst for change. If we don't use video to see what we are doing when we interact, there is a real danger we will waste our time by not focusing on the most important area for improvement.

IDENTIFY (B)

Analyze the video using a reflection form.

After video recording a conversation, you need to analyze it. You might want to look carefully at how you listen, ask questions, build connections, or some other habit. To improve in any particular area, look at your current reality with focused attention.

To assist with your analysis of your video, reflection forms are included at the end of each of the 10 Habits chapters. The forms are tools you can use to look at your video with focused attention to see what you otherwise might not have seen.

IDENTIFY (C)

Identify a goal.
To bring focus to your coaching, you need to identify a goal. Goals focus attention, they provide a destination to strive for, and they help us identify when have we arrived at our destination.

LEARN

Learn the applicable Better Conversations Habit.

After you've decided on a goal, you'll need to consider which of the 10 Better Conversations Habits to learn in order to help you achieve your goal and then set about learning that habit inside out. If you determine that you would like to be a better listener, study the chapter on Habit 2, Listen. You'll learn effective strategies that will help you to listen well. You might create your own checklists to review and commit to memory to help you as you move forward.

IMPROVE

Monitor progress toward your goal.

The Improve part of the Improvement Cycle is where you tweak a goal, reconsider the goal, possibly create an entirely new goal, and begin the cycle of monitoring your progress toward your goal all over again until you gain mastery. For example, an instructional coach who wants to have better conversations might video record herself during coaching sessions and determine that she needs to be more dialogical. She might set the goal that her collaborating teachers will do at least 50% of the thinking during coaching conversations, and then use the dialogue strategies to do less telling and more collaborative reflection. Then, she can continue to video record her coaching conversations and use the reflection forms to identify what she is doing well and where she needs to improve as she strive to become more dialogical.

After you've set a goal, and you're gathering data by video recording and analyzing your conversations with the help of the reflection forms, you may realize your first attempts won't always hit the target. This is where you make adjustments as you learn from your video. Perhaps you realize you need to change your goal because you discover a more foundational challenge than you had first anticipated. For example, you may think you don't listen well, but you realize you aren't listening well because you've not mastered a more foundational habit such as building emotional connections or being nonjudgmental.

There are as many variations here as there are people. This will be unique to you, and it may not look exactly the same twice.

How Should I Use This Book?

////////////////////////

As you work through *The Reflection Guide to Better Conversations*, you may use it in different ways. If you find yourself in a Better Conversations Workshop, this book will stand in the place of slides. Perhaps you are reading *Better Conversations: Coaching Ourselves and Each Other to Be More Credible, Caring, and Connected*, and you wish to work through the content and practice it on a deeper level by beginning to coach yourself. You might be in a book study group comprised of peers and friends and use this book to guide you as you practice coaching one another. Similarly, teams of professionals may use it to coach themselves as they implement the ideas found in *Better Conversations*. And, of course, instructional coaches may work through the book and use the tools to assist them as they come alongside instructors and guide them through the coaching process.

Part 1

BELIEFS

The Six Beliefs of Better Conversations
//////////////////

The six beliefs that stand at the heart of better conversations are the following:

1. I see others as equal partners in conversations.
2. I believe people should have a lot of autonomy.
3. I want to hear what others have to say.
4. I don't judge my conversation partners.
5. Conversation should be back and forth.
6. Conversation should be life-giving.

To learn and internalize the Better Conversation Beliefs and Habits, we need to become aware of what Michael Polanyi refers to as tacit knowledge (the beliefs and habits we embrace without even knowing it), learn explicit knowledge (the beliefs and habits described in this book), and then practice them until they become tacit (habits we use all the time when we are engaged in conversations).

What Are Your Beliefs About Communication?

The journey toward having better conversations is actually a journey toward authenticity. Both beliefs and actions (referred to as habits, which will be addressed in detail in part 2 of this workbook) matter. Authenticity is an alignment of who we say we are and believe with how we behave. Understanding our beliefs and our habits is not just a way of being authentic; understanding our beliefs and habits is also vitally important for improving how we communicate.

Perhaps the major finding we've gathered from reviewing more than 1,000 Communication Learning forms is that when people watch video recordings of their conversations, they are usually very surprised to see that how they act is quite different from how they thought they acted. What we believe we do and what we really do are often not the same. We can believe in listening and still talk too much. Our actions can be inconsistent with our beliefs.

Knowing what we believe is a vital first step for change. Our beliefs give shape to who we are and what we do. We can hold them as individuals, or we can hold them collectively as part of the culture of an organization.

In the end, our behavior—not our words—will nearly always reveal what we truly, however subconsciously, believe. Because ideas and beliefs about the world drive behavior, we start by giving careful, mindful thought to what it is we believe to be true about what makes for better communication.

"Behavior is the mirror in which everyone shows their image."
/////////////////

JOHANN WOLFGANG VON GOETHE

The following section will introduce six foundational beliefs about communication, and will provide you with prompts, questions, and activities to guide you as you thoughtfully decide what ideas drive the way you communicate.

We are not slaves to our beliefs. We get to choose them, but to do so, we must surface our current beliefs and then consider what alternative beliefs might better describe who we are and who we want to be.

As we work through *Better Conversations*, it's important to understand the difference between top-down communication and partnership communication. Jot down in this chart the differences you see as you read.

TOP-DOWN COMMUNICATION	PARTNERSHIP COMMUNICATION

I SEE OTHERS AS
EQUAL PARTNERS.

BELIEF

////////////////////

1

"It is amazing how often we move to positions of power when we are not consciously aware of the need to stay in good communication with others."

////////////////

MARILYN ALLEN
Instructional Coach

When I choose to have a better conversation, rather than a top-down conversation, I bring my full humanity to the conversation—all my ideas, passions, emotions, and confusions—and I expect and desire that my conversation partner will do the same. During a better conversation, I see the people with whom I'm interacting as people who should be valued, whose opinion matters, who can think for themselves, and who make their own decisions. A better conversation, as Paulo Freire would say, is a mutually humanizing conversation. Better conversations make both of us better. When I see others as equals, I see them having the same value as I do—they count the same. If I work from the core principle of equality, others should never feel that I see myself as superior to them. Indeed, in a better conversation, I intentionally look to see my conversation partners' strengths—and communicate in some way that I know them.

Where Do You Stand on Equality?

Edgar Schein explains that when people position themselves as superior, they create an unequal relationship that inhibits communication and professional learning. According to Schein, people only feel conversations have been successful when they are given the status they deserve. Often, the reason people resist ideas in top-down conversations is that they are not getting the status they feel they deserve.

Schein highlights three critical aspects of equality. Spend some time reflecting on your experiences, beliefs, and actions regarding these.

STATUS

Whenever people feel they aren't getting the status they deserve in a conversation, they stop listening or resist what is being offered. For that reason, if we want to have impact, we need to keep our need for status in check.

Have you ever protected your need for status by assuming an expert or authoritative position and potentially disregarded others?

....
....
....
....

BUY-IN

In schools we hear people say, "I just need to get buy-in to my ideas." When you see others as equals, the concept of buy-in no longer makes sense. When we strive for buy-in, we work from the assumption that we have the best ideas and others should just do what we say. In contrast, when we believe in equality, we assume we will have a better solution if everyone's brains are involved. Also, when we see others as equals, we recognize that professionals expect to be involved in the thinking, and when they aren't, there is a good chance they will resist.

Are you often convinced that you have the best solution for problems? If so, has it been difficult to work well with others?

....
....
....
....

What are challenges to collectively solving problems instead of persuading others to buy-in to your solution?

....
....
....
....
....

EXPERTISE

This is a complex variable when it comes to Better Conversations. On the one hand, if others are going to listen to us and trust us, they need to see us as competent and credible. On the other hand, if we push our opinions rather than listen, we won't learn and we'll probably engender resistance (Miller & Rollnick, 2002). To be heard, we need to have something of value to say, but if we are always talking, others won't listen. If we believe others are equal, we probably should listen to them first before we share what we have to say.

Have you ever felt the need to defend your expertise or authority in a conversation? If so, how did you do it and how did it feel?

....
....
....
....
....

Have there been times when it was difficult for you to recognize others' expertise in conversations or decisions? If so, what made it difficult?

....
....
....
....

REMINDER:
Beliefs are complex. Your perspective may not align with this belief 100%. It is more important that you are honest with yourself and thoughtfully consider what your perspective is.

CONSIDER

Which statement most reflects your current thoughts about this belief (treating others as equal partners)?

○ I DISAGREE   ○ I'M SKEPTICAL   ○ I'M NOT SURE   ○ IT IS HELPFUL   ○ IT IS ESSENTIAL

On a scale of 1-10, how important is it for you to get better at treating others as equal partners in conversations?

UNIMPORTANT ○─○─○─○─○─○─○─○─○─○ CRITICAL
                  1 2 3 4 5 6 7 8 9 10

REFLECT

To treat someone as an equal is to treat her as counting the same as you. To give someone status is, most simply, to give her respectful regard and to allow her contribution to the conversation to have the same weight as you give your own. What might it actually look and sound like when we intentionally give another person status—that is, respectful regard as opposed to thinly veiled disregard?

....
....
....
....
....
....

Trying to get buy-in is a top-down communication tactic that disrespects another person because it violates the principle of equality—the idea that others' opinions and ideas need to count the same as your own. While you may have an idea you believe effectively addresses a common challenge, how might you present it in a way that shows other people what you have in mind yet invites them to brainstorm along with you? If we become attached emotionally to our own ideas, it becomes hard to collaborate with others. What types of things could you say to yourself (reframing your inner monologue) to create a genuine interest in others' ideas?

....
....
....
....
....
....
....

An expert is respected when he or she engenders trust, is competent, credible, and is willing to listen before speaking. Expertise isn't solely about being a master in your content area, it is also about being a master at treating others respectfully. What will others see and hear as you continue to commit to creating expertise born of humility and regard for others?

....
....
....
....
....
....
....

LOOKING AT MY BELIEFS:

I see others as equal partners in conversations.

//

To understand how it might look and feel to honor or violate the belief that others should be equal partners in conversations, the following examples of top-down communication and partnership communication are provided. Use this simple scale to help gauge the alignment you currently possess between your beliefs and your behavior (authenticity). The higher total score, the more oriented you are toward partnership communication. The lower total score, the more oriented you are toward top-down communication.

TOP-DOWN PRACTICES		**PARTNERSHIP PRACTICES**
It is OK to manipulate others to get what I want.	1 2 3 4 5 6 7 8 9 10	I make sure I treat others as deserving of status.
I want people to "buy-in" to my ideas.	1 2 3 4 5 6 7 8 9 10	I want an outcome everyone embraces even if it's not my own.
It is of paramount importance that others recognize my expertise.	1 2 3 4 5 6 7 8 9 10	I am more concerned with recognizing others' expertise than I am about them recognizing mine.

Total Score

What surprises you? What pleases you? Are you where you would like to be? What would you like to change?

....

....

....

....

....

....

....

....

....

I WANT TO HEAR WHAT OTHERS HAVE TO SAY.

"There is a lot of difference between listening and hearing."

//////////////

G.K. CHESTERTON

People want to be heard, and too often they are

not. Marcus Buckingham and Curt Coffman reviewed surveys of over a million

employees and 90-minute interviews of over 80,000 managers to identify the

characteristics of a strong workplace. In *First Break All The Rules: What the*

World's Greatest Managers Do Differently (1999), the researchers synthesized

their findings into 12 questions, with the idea that employees who answer yes

to all 12 questions are more likely to be engaged and motivated. The seventh

question on the list was, "At work, do my opinions seem to count?" Employees

who are engaged by their work report that what they have to say is important

to their organizations.

What Do You Believe About Wanting to Hear What Others Have to Say?

We can enter into conversations by asking questions and making sure we understand what others are saying before we give our opinions. By temporarily setting aside our own opinions, we can really hear what others have to say and powerfully demonstrate that we respect others' perspectives. When we listen with empathy to others' ideas, thoughts, and concerns, we communicate that others' lives are important and meaningful.

FOCUS

If we want to hear what others have to say, we need to make sure that the conversation is focused on others at least 50% of the time. This means we frequently withhold comments and ask questions that keep the focus on others. Simple questions such as these can go a long way toward making sure the conversation is focused on others at least as much as it is focused on us:

- » What do you think about _____?
- » How do you feel about _____?
- » What would you do?
- » What could make this easier or better?

Is there someone who shows deep interest in your life? How do they show that interest in a conversation with you?

....
....
....
....
....
....

PRESENCE

Being fully present to others is a sign of respect and, of course, is necessary to really hear what others have to say. This means that we put aside our thoughts and devices and focus on those with whom we are talking. Not every conversation is the same, and it may not be as important to be fully present when someone talks about their fantasy hockey team as it is when someone talks with us about the challenges they are facing raising their teenage son. Too often though, we are distracted, and by being present we can learn more and communicate genuine respect.

Many people in our study reported they had to turn off their phones, shut down their computers, and not look at their watches to make sure they kept their attention on others. When volunteers in our

RECOMMENDED READING:
Thinking for a Living
//////////////
THOMAS H. DAVENPORT

First, Break All The Rules
//////////////
MARCUS BUCKINGHAM AND
CURT COFFMAN

Making Hope Happen
//////////////
SHANE LOPEZ

Student Voice:
The Instrument of Change
//////////////
RUSSELL J. QUAGLIA AND
MICHAEL J. CORSO

"The saddest part about being human is not paying attention. Presence is the gift of life."
//////////////
STEPHEN LEVINE

study watched video of themselves in conversation, they saw that their technology was more distracting than they realized. Janet Attallah, for example, saw that just looking at her watch for a second essentially ended a conversation with a student. Technology can help us communicate in many ways, but it can also distract us from paying attention to the people right in front of us.

Are there habits that distract you from paying attention to others?

....

....

....

....

....

Are there habits you can adopt that would remind you to give others more attention in conversation?

....

....

....

....

....

TIMING

Many people in our study said they had to prepare themselves and clear their minds of their own thoughts before they could really hear others. One way people do this is to make sure that when they have a serious conversation, they choose the right time. If they are harboring angry or negative thoughts, they probably should wait and have the conversation when they can truly listen with an open mind and heart.

Think of a time and a place where you had a conversation that didn't go very well. Was there anything you could done to so it would have resulted in a more constructive conversation?

....

....

....

....

....

....

....

....

REMINDER:
Beliefs are complex. Your perspective may not align with this belief 100%. It is more important that you are honest with yourself and thoughtfully consider what your perspective is.

CONSIDER

Which statement most reflects your current thoughts about this belief (hearing what others have to say)?

○ I DISAGREE   ○ I'M SKEPTICAL   ○ I'M NOT SURE   ○ IT IS HELPFUL   ○ IT IS ESSENTIAL

On a scale of 1-10, how important is it for you to get better at hearing what others have to say?

UNIMPORTANT ○—○—○—○—○—○—○—○—○—○ CRITICAL
1 2 3 4 5 6 7 8 9 10

REFLECTIONS

Think about a conversation you recently experienced. What percent of the time were you focused on yourself? Are you in the habit of mindlessly offering unsolicited commentary, or are you comfortable withholding your comments?

....
....
....
....
....
....
....
....
....

In addition to the obvious things that can distract us from being present to another person, a more subtle distracter is how we practice and approach power. If structural or positional power is confused with real power, we are likely to create an environment where people will be less likely to be open with us. How have you seen confusion about power at work in others? What does it look like when people are confused about power?

....
....
....
....
....
....
....
....
....
....

Appropriately timing conversation is an art and an expression of grace. Do you believe it is important for a conversation to be unhurried so that people will not feel pressured or rushed into a decision? What about your personal energy? Have you had the time you need to clear your mind of negative thoughts, so you can approach your conversation partners with humility and openness? How important is it to respect the time constraints in others' schedules when considering the timing of an important conversation?

REFLECTIONS

LOOKING AT MY BELIEFS:

I want to hear what others have to say.

To understand how it might look and feel to honor or violate the belief that you want to hear what people have to say, the following examples of what it looks like to use top-down communication and partnership communication are provided. Use this simple scale to help gauge the alignment you currently possess between your beliefs and your behavior (authenticity). The higher total score, the more oriented you are toward partnership communication. The lower total score, the more oriented you are toward top-down communication.

TOP-DOWN PRACTICES		**PARTNERSHIP PRACTICES**
I do most of the talking during conversations.	1 2 3 4 5 6 7 8 9 10	Others do most of the talking during conversations.
It is OK if I multi-task during conversations.	1 2 3 4 5 6 7 8 9 10	I am fully present when I have conversations.
I don't worry about how anger or negative feelings interfere with my ability to listen.	1 2 3 4 5 6 7 8 9 10	I try to make sure I'm ready to listen before I have an important conversation.

Total Score ☐

What surprises you? What pleases you? Are you where you would like to be? What would you like to change?

....
....
....
....
....
....
....
....

I BELIEVE OTHER PEOPLE SHOULD HAVE A LOT OF AUTONOMY.

BELIEF

///////////////////////.

3

"The proper question is not, 'how can people motivate others?' but rather, 'how can people create the conditions within which others will motivate themselves?'"

///////////////////,

EDWARD DECI
Why We Do What We Do

When we see those we communicate with as equal partners, we inevitably see them as autonomous people who should make their own choices. Partners don't tell their partners what to do. Furthermore, taking away choice is dehumanizing. As Freire (1970) says, "Freedom ... is the indispensable condition for the quest for human completion ... without freedom [we] cannot exist authentically" (p. 31). Similarly, Peter Block (1993) emphasizes the primacy of choice: "Partners each have a right to say no. Saying no is the fundamental way we have of differentiating ourselves. To take away my right to say no is to claim sovereignty over me ... If we cannot say no, then saying yes has no meaning" (pp. 30–31).

Do You Believe People Should Have a Lot of Autonomy?

Teachers are just like everyone else—none of us likes to be told what to do. Edward Deci and Richard Ryan have dedicated their lives to studying motivation, and one of their major findings is that people are rarely motivated by other people's plans for them. As Deci writes in *Why We Do What We Do: Understanding Self-Motivation* (1995),

> *Control is an easy answer. It ... sounds tough, so it feels reassuring to people who believe things have gone awry ... however, it has become increasingly clear that the approach simply does not work... the widespread reliance on rewards and punishments to motivate responsibility has failed to yield the desired results. Indeed, mounting evidence suggests that these so-called solutions, based on the principle of rigid authority, are exacerbating rather than ameliorating the problems.*

> *The proper question is not, "how can people motivate others?" but rather, "how can people create the conditions within which others will motivate themselves?"*

Respecting others' needs for autonomy is both a practical and a good thing to do. It is practical because people will not be motivated to change or embrace what we have to say unless they have real choices. On the other hand, trying to control others is dehumanizing. The surest way to ensure that someone doesn't do something, whether they are 6 or 66 years old, is to tell them they have to do it.

"When you insist, they will resist."
/////////////,
TIMOTHY GALLWEY

Autonomy is as important for young people as it is for adults. As Jim Fay and David Funk have written in *Teaching with Love and Logic: Taking Control of the Classroom* (1995), "We all want to have some control over our lives and when we feel we are losing that control we will fight to the end to get it back" (p. 69). Recognizing the importance of control, Fay and Funk to identify shared control as one of the four key principles of their love and logic approach. They write that "when we allow kids to have some control over their own learning, they often amaze even the most experienced teacher" (p.212).

Has there been a time when you didn't have autonomy or shared control of a setting? How did that affect you, positively or negatively?

....

....

....

....

....

....

....

....

....

CHOICE

Central to respecting others' autonomy is, of course, ensuring they have the freedom to choose in most situations. In conversations, this means that although we clearly state what we have to say, we speak in a way that is provisional and allows others the freedom to choose what they believe. This means we say something like, "You might see this differently, but what I've found is ..." rather than "Everybody knows the truth is ..." When we don't force our opinions on others, they are much more likely to embrace what we share.

"Saying no is the fundamental way we have of differentiating ourselves. To take away my right to say no is to claim sovereignty over me … If we cannot say no, then saying yes has no meaning."
//////////////,
PETER BLOCK

In your conversations, is it natural for you to give others permission to choose or believe differently than you?

....

....

....

....

....

....

What are some ways to share your beliefs or ideas provisionally, allowing others to have a choice?

....

....

....

....

....

....

....

DECISION MAKING

When we respect others' autonomy, we don't do the thinking for them. Our goal, in fact, should be to think with others rather than for them. We can accomplish mutual decision-making by finding ways to move away from positional conversation to dialogical conversations. A simple way to do this is to look for a third way to make decisions. Rather than engaging in a win-lose conversation, we honor autonomy by establishing a third side for the conversation to help with thinking (Ury, 2000). A third side can be an objective standard, a third thing that both of us view (such as a video recording of a classroom) or a third person. We can also foster thinking together by using processes that are structured to lead to mutual decisions. The instructional coaching model that I've described (Knight, 2015) is designed to lead to powerful outcomes while positioning the teacher being coached as the primary decision maker.

Are there times when someone has not given you the option to make decisions for yourself professionally? How did that affect you?

....

....

....

....

....

OUTCOMES

Being in control, for most of us, feels good. The opposite is also true, especially when we are responsible for leading a classroom, a school, or a system. One way to be in control is to get the outcomes that we want. The trouble is when our need for control runs up against another's need for autonomy, we often struggle to come up with any kind of mutually satisfactory outcome.

Since the work in schools deals with moral action—making a difference in the lives of children—people can intentionally or unintentionally confuse their need for control with what's best for kids. That is, perhaps the outcome I want for children also happens to be something I control. Part of honoring others' involves letting them be the master of many aspects of their lives. It also means we scrutinize our motives to make sure that we aren't using the rationale of doing what is good as an excuse for doing what we want.

RECOMMENDED READING:
Drive
/////////////,
DANIEL H. PINK

Are there times when you have made a decision for someone for "their own good?" If so, was the outcome satisfactory?

....

....

....

....

....

CONSIDER

Which statement most reflects your current thoughts about this belief (giving others autonomy)?

○   ○   ○   ○   ○
I DISAGREE   I'M SKEPTICAL   I'M NOT SURE   IT IS HELPFUL   IT IS ESSENTIAL

On a scale of 1-10, how important is it for you to get better at giving others autonomy?

UNIMPORTANT ○─○─○─○─○─○─○─○─○─○ CRITICAL
            1 2 3 4 5 6 7 8 9 10

REMINDER:
Beliefs are complex. Your perspective may not align with this belief 100%. It is more important that you are honest with yourself and thoughtfully consider what your perspective is.

REFLECTIONS

Is it possible to name a fear which holds you back from being able to allow others choice and the freedom to be or feel different than you? In naming that fear, can you then address it in a way that makes your conversations more tolerant?

....

....

....

....

....

....

What are some creative ways in which you might invite others into a mutual decision-making conversation? Think about ways you could generate excitement within yourself for this conversation by being eager to learn from others' perspectives.

....

....

....

....

....

....

....

Often, when we feel compelled to be controlling, it may be a sign we are worried about something we've not recognized. It also may be that we are simply crunched for time, and dictating seems most efficient.

What is the fear that is flying under the radar, and how can you address that and allow greater autonomy for your conversation partner? If you find it's less about fear and more about not having enough time, consider Monty Roberts' words: "... if you act like you only have a few minutes," it can take all day to accomplish a change, whereas "if you act like you have all day," it may only take a few minutes. What would it look like to converse at a truly humane speed?

LOOKING AT MY BELIEFS:

I believe people should have a lot of autonomy.

//

To understand how it might look and feel to honor or violate the belief that people should have a lot of autonomy, the following examples of top-down communication and partnership communication are provided. Use this simple scale to help gauge the alignment you currently possess between your beliefs and your behavior (authenticity). The higher total score, the more oriented you are toward partnership communication. The lower total score, the more oriented you are toward top-down communication.

TOP-DOWN PRACTICES   **PARTNERSHIP PRACTICES**

People should do what they are told.

○—○—○—○—○—○—○—○—○—○
1 2 3 4 5 6 7 8 9 10

Telling people what to do without giving them choices creates resistance.

I do most of the thinking for others.

○—○—○—○—○—○—○—○—○—○
1 2 3 4 5 6 7 8 9 10

I think with others.

I want my own outcomes.

○—○—○—○—○—○—○—○—○—○
1 2 3 4 5 6 7 8 9 10

I want the best outcome.

Total Score [   ]

What surprises you? What pleases you? Are you where you would like to be? What would you like to change?

....
....
....
....
....
....
....
....

I DON'T JUDGE OTHERS.

4

> *"It's not our differences that divide us. It's our judgments about each other."*
>
> ///////////////,
>
> **MARGARET WHEATLEY**
> *Turning to One Another*

When people judge others, they destroy any pretense of equality. If I judge you as having done something well or poorly, by doing that very act I put myself one-up and put you one-down. To be nonjudg-

> *"There are many ways we can roll our eyes that don't involve our eyes."*
>
> ///////////////,
>
> **MICHAEL FULLAN**

mental does not mean we ignore reality. Certainly, when we are engaged with the world and especially when we are in leadership positions, we need to use our ability to discern reality. Being nonjudgmental means we don't share our perceptions in a way that diminishes others. When we are nonjudgmental, we don't roll our eyes when we talk about another person.

What Do You Believe About Being Nonjudgmental?

Judgment destroys any pretense of equality and destroys what Dennis and Michelle Reina call "communication trust."

Communication trust is key to creating and maintaining a nonjudgmental environment, which facilitates better conversations. Conversational trust develops, Dennis and Michelle Reina say, "when people feel comfortable and safe enough to share their perceptions regarding one another's perceptions without repercussions. They trust they will not suffer the consequences of retaliation because they spoke the truth" (p.47).

There are a few simple things you can do to be nonjudgmental. First, you can listen without assumptions and without prejudging your conversation partner. Second, you can begin to let go of the desire to give unsolicited advice. Third, you can practice letting go of having to be right.

ASSUMPTIONS

To be nonjudgmental we should listen to others without assumption and without prejudging their comments. If we jump to conclusions about what other people say, chances are they will notice and consequently be less open.

Think of someone who jumps to conclusions about your thoughts or beliefs. How does it affect your relationship with them?

....
....
....
....
....
....

GIVING ADVICE

To be nonjudgmental we need to let go of the desire to give advice. For some reason, many of us have an almost uncontrollable desire to tell others how they should go about their business. However, in almost all cases, our partners don't want advice unless they specifically ask for it. What people want is someone who is nonjudgmental, listens with empathy, and values their ideas.

"Communication trust is the willingness to share information, tell the truth, admit mistakes, maintain confidentiality, give and receive constructive feedback, and speak with good purpose." (p. 34).
////////////////
DENNIS AND MICHELE REINA
Trust and Betrayal in The Workplace

"*If you start a conversation with the assumption that you are right or that you must win, obviously it is difficult to talk.*"
////////////////
WENDELL BERRY

Are there times when you have valued someone's advice? Was there
anything about the way in which it was delivered that made you
more open to that advice?

....

....

....

....

....

Have you ever received unwanted advice? How did it affect you?

....

....

....

....

....

KNOWING WHAT IS RIGHT

Part of being judgmental is our tendency to be overly certain that
we are right. When we are judgmental, we tend to feel there is only
one right way, and that happens to be our way. For that reason, we
spend a lot of time explaining why we are right and why others are
wrong. When we take the nonjudgmental approach, we believe that
others might actually have better ideas than ours.

Think about times when you have learned from a student. How did
you feel? How do you think they felt?

....

....

....

....

....

Are there times when you force your ideas on others? Do you
achieve what you want out of the conversation or interactions?

....

....

....

....

....

CONSIDER

Which statement most reflects your current thoughts about this belief (not judging partners)?

○   ○   ○   ○   ○

I DISAGREE   I'M SKEPTICAL   I'M NOT SURE   IT IS HELPFUL   IT IS ESSENTIAL

On a scale of 1-10, how important is it for you to get better at not judging conversation partners?

UNIMPORTANT ○—○—○—○—○—○—○—○—○—○ CRITICAL
                1   2   3   4   5   6   7   8   9   10

REFLECTIONS

We all know the old adage about making assumptions. In order to stop making incorrect assumptions, try to recognize a fear or other underlying disconnect in your thinking which could be feeding the need to make assumptions. Could this be addressed in such a way that would free you up internally and help you objectively hear your conversation partner without making snap judgments about him or her?

....

....

....

....

....

....

....

....

....

....

What drives you to offer unwanted advice? Is it a fear of looking like you don't have it all together? A need to try to fix things for your partner? Or is it a mindless, bad habit that has taken root? How can you check yourself before you give advice?

....

....

....

....

....

....

....

....

....

....

Sometimes it is really hard to accept that we might be wrong. Other times we have objective evidence that we hold a correct position. Either way, if we are insistent upon one way (our own!) and don't allow that others may have a better course of action, we shut down what could have been a better conversation. Consider how sometimes our own way might be the right way, but in reality it is one of many "right" ways. How can keeping an open mind in this regard help you be less judgemental about others and thereby enrich your relationships?

REFLECTIONS

LOOKING AT MY BELIEFS:

I don't judge my conversation partners.

///

To understand how it might look and feel to honor or violate the belief that it is important to not judge conversation partners, the following examples of top-down communication and partnership communication are provided. Use this simple scale to help gauge the alignment you currently possess between your beliefs and your behavior (authenticity). The higher total score, the more oriented you are toward partnership communication. The lower total score, the more oriented you are toward top-down communication.

TOP-DOWN PRACTICES		**PARTNERSHIP PRACTICES**
I have a habit of assuming a lot about what other people say.	O—O—O—O—O—O—O—O—O—O 1 2 3 4 5 6 7 8 9 10	I listen to people without making assumptions.
I don't hesitate to give advice even if it is not requested.	O—O—O—O—O—O—O—O—O—O 1 2 3 4 5 6 7 8 9 10	I never give unsolicited advice.
Other people need to accept that my way is almost always the right way.	O—O—O—O—O—O—O—O—O—O 1 2 3 4 5 6 7 8 9 10	I seek others' opinions since they could easily have better ideas than mine.

Total Score [   ]

What surprises you? What pleases you? Are you where you would like to be? What would you like to change?

....

....

....

....

....

....

....

....

CONVERSATION SHOULD BE BACK-AND-FORTH.

5

"Dialogue is non-confrontational communication where both partners are willing to learn from the other and therefore leads much farther into finding new ground together."

//////////////////

SCILLA ELWORTHY

A better conversation is one that is created by everyone in the conversation. This back-and-forth, co-constructed form of conversation we can refer to as a dialogue. Seeing conversation as a two-way interaction is to live out our true respect for our conversation partners in the way we communicate. During a better conversation, my conversation partners and I become more thoughtful, creative, and alive when we talk in ways that open up rather than shut down our thinking and talking. A belief that conversation should be back and forth is almost inevitable if we adopt the other Better Conversation Beliefs. If I see others as equals, if I want to hear what they have to say, if I recognize that people are going to make their autonomous decisions about what I share, then inevitably I will assume that a better conversation is one that is created by everyone in the conversation.

Do You Believe Conversations Should be Back-and-Forth?

When we practice conversation as a two-way interaction, we live out our true respect for the people with whom we communicate. In fact, when we see others as complete human beings, and we respect them as autonomous people rather than objects to be manipulated, we almost always embrace back-and-forth interactions.

Paulo Freire suggests that five conditions are necessary for two-way dialogue to happen:

» Humility
» Hope
» Faith
» Critical Thinking
» Love

When these underlying conditions are not what guide dialogue, it becomes easy to manipulate, focus on only our own purpose, and not learn from others. These qualities are detrimental to true dialogue.

MANIPULATION

When we embrace the belief that conversation should be back-and-forth, we do it because we genuinely see others as partners in a conversation and not just as objects to motivate, shape, or sell to. In some situations manipulation may be necessary, especially adult-to-child situations such as when a teacher skillfully offers choices to get a student back on task, but manipulation is inconsistent with seeing others as equal.

The alternative to a manipulative conversation can be, as Emily Manning wrote on her reflection form, a beautiful thing. During a back-and-forth or dialogical conversation, all parties are engaged and shaped by a free and honest discussion. In *On Dialogue*, David Bohm writes that dialogue is a form of communication where meaning moves back and forth between and through people.

Think about a time when you felt manipulated in a conversation. What do you wish the other person would have done differently?

....
....
....
....
....

"The picture or image that this derivation suggests is of a stream of meaning flowing among and through us and between us ... out of which will emerge some new understanding. It's something new, which may not have been in the starting point at all. It's something creative. And this shared meaning is the 'glue' or 'cement' that holds people and societies together." (p. 1).
/////////////////

DAVID BOHM
On Dialogue

PURPOSE

Sometimes the purpose of communication is to make sure that our audience receives the message we want them to receive. A Better Conversation, however, typically has a different purpose. During Better Conversations, we try to listen as much as we talk, and learn as much as we teach. When conversation is back and forth, all parties are shaped by the brainpower of everyone in the conversation.

Who are the people in your life you learn from most in conversation? What is it about those conversations that makes them enriching?

....
....
....
....
....
....
....

LEARNING

Back-and-forth conversations are important because those we communicate with usually know a lot about what they do. Not listening to what they say is simply poor thinking. Teachers, for example, who work directly with students often have profound insights into what works best for those students. And students themselves have the most intimate understanding of their own experiences. For that reason, we should seek out others' insights, rather than just be telling. When we believe in back-and-forth conversations, one reason is that we want to learn from others.

"Education is a kind of continuing dialogue, and a dialogue assumes different points of view."
//////////////
ROBERT M. HUTCHINS

What are ways you can gain insight into another's experience or perspective during a conversation?

....
....
....
....
....
....
....

Which statement most reflects your current thoughts about this belief (conversations should be back and forth)?

○   ○   ○   ○   ○
I DISAGREE   I'M SKEPTICAL   I'M NOT SURE   IT IS HELPFUL   IT IS ESSENTIAL

On a scale of 1-10, how important is it for you to get better at facilitating conversations that are back and forth?

UNIMPORTANT ○—○—○—○—○—○—○—○—○—○ CRITICAL
                    1   2   3   4   5   6   7   8   9   10

REFLECTIONS

What might tempt you to be manipulative? Do those reasons reflect a subconscious fear or unnamed pressure which you could specifically address and so destroy manipulation at its root?

....

....

....

....

....

....

....

....

....

....

As a professional, you often need to have a clear purpose or (shared) agenda for certain conversations. However, rigid adherence to the agenda is detrimental when it comes at the expense of the loss of others' voices. What are some creative ways you can allow for true dialogue while keeping the conversation on track?

....

....

....

....

....

....

....

....

....

....

....

....

REMINDER:
Beliefs are complex. Your perspective may not align with this belief 100%. It is more important that you are honest with yourself and thoughtfully consider what your perspective is.

52 | BETTER CONVERSATIONS: COMPANION BOOK

Do you believe your students have the most intimate understanding
of their experiences at school? In what ways do you learn from them
and give them voice in meaningful, powerful ways?

REFLECTIONS

LOOKING AT MY BELIEFS:

Conversation should be back and forth.

To understand how it might look and feel to honor or violate the belief that conversations should be back and forth, the following examples of top-down communication and partnership communication are provided. Use this simple scale to help gauge the alignment you currently possess between your beliefs and your behavior (authenticity). The higher total score, the more oriented you are toward partnership communication. The lower total score, the more oriented you are toward top-down communication.

TOP-DOWN PRACTICES | **PARTNERSHIP PRACTICES**

It is OK to manipulate others to get what I want. 1 2 3 4 5 6 7 8 9 10 I see others as fully human and strive to never manipulate them.

Communication is about making sure others receive my message. 1 2 3 4 5 6 7 8 9 10 Communication is about two or more people being shaped by the brain power of everyone in a conversation.

I'm only concerned about instructing others. 1 2 3 4 5 6 7 8 9 10 I always want to learn from others.

Total Score

What surprises you? What pleases you? Are you where you would like to be? What would you like to change?

....
....
....
....
....
....
....
....

CONVERSATION SHOULD BE LIFE-GIVING.

6

"Our duty is to encourage everyone to live up to his own highest idea, and strive at the same time to make the ideal as near as possible to the truth."

///////////////

SWAMI VIVEKANANDA

When I believe conversation should be life-giving, I go into conversations expecting that my conversation partners and I will leave conversations feeling more alive for having experienced them. People usually feel better when they engage in conversations about topics that matter and when their ideas are heard and acted upon. Furthermore, when people come together to set and achieve goals, a bond can come into being, a deep affection can grow, and important life-long friendships can develop.

Do You Believe That Conversation Should Be Life-Giving?

Life-giving conversations should increase our well-being, inspire us, impart positive energy, and protect our self-esteem and identity. The DNA of a life-giving conversation is encouragement. It is the will to use our words to call forth the highest good inside another person. Better conversationalists know that what he or she communicates is what they build—not only in the life of another person but in their greater environment. In contrast, life-alienating conversations are full of moralistic judgments, comparisons, demands, denial, labels, and verbal abusiveness.

Simply put, life-giving conversations are engaging, they are positively energizing, and they increase our sense of well-being.

ENGAGEMENT

Every so often we have conversations that touch us so deeply and so positively that they change our lives. During those interactions, we are almost always deeply engaged in what is being said. We won't have life-giving conversations by just going through the motions. Better Conversations fully capture everyone's attention.

We will be more engaged in conversations if we choose to talk about things that matter. The Better Conversations Beliefs and Habits make this much more likely. When we care about what others say, and respect others as equals, we are more likely to find ourselves talking about important topics. Indeed, if we are not engaged during conversations, chances are we are not living out the Better Conversation Beliefs.

Think of a conversation you have had where you were completely engaged. How did it make you feel? Did time seem to fly? What life-giving elements created the engaging atmosphere?

....

....

....

....

....

....

ENERGY

Not all important conversations energize us, of course. Sometimes after we talk about difficult challenges people face, we feel exhausted. While such difficult or painful conversations may not energize us, they usually leave us feeling we have used our time productively.

More typically, Better Conversations increase our energy. When those we talk with hear what we are saying, when we think together with others about important topics, and when we feel affirmed by those with whom we talk, we usually feel energized. At their best, conversations help us better understand what matters, what we need to do, and why we are the right person for doing what we need to do—and that usually means we are enthusiastic about taking on whatever life brings us.

Have you recently come away from a conversation where you felt uplifted and energized—like you were better able and excited to take on life? What life-giving elements were present? Which elements did your partner contribute? How did you contribute?

....

....

....

....

Alternatively, some conversations can leave you feeling like all the psychological air has been sucked out of the room. They're depressing and leave you depleted. What types of attitudes and subjects create these kinds of life-alienating conversations?

....

....

....

....

....

WELL-BEING

Conversations where we do not feel we are heard, or worse, where we feel judged and diminished, can decrease happiness, energy, and well-being. At their worst, the most destructive conversations do more than decrease our energy; they damage our self-esteem and identity. If we are experiencing such destructive conversations, we'd be wise to learn more about verbal abuse and act quickly to remove ourselves from situations where we are abused. (See Patricia Evans, *The Verbally Abusive Relationship, Expanded Third Edition: How to Recognize it and How to Respond*, 2010.)

Better Conversations should increase our well-being. Martin Seligman, has popularized the research on positive psychology. In his book, *Flourish: A Visionary New Understanding of Happiness and*

RECOMMENDED READING:

Nonviolent Communication, A Language of Life
//////////////

MARSHALL B. ROSENBERG, PH.D

Well-being (2012), he identifies five elements that should be in place for us to experience well-being—(a) positive emotion, (b) engagement, (c) positive relationships, (d) meaning, and (e) accomplishment or achievement. Each of these elements should also be in place in Better Conversations. When we learn with other people, talk with them about our passions, feel encouraged, seen, and heard, we should experience more well-being. Better Conversations should make our lives better.

Consider a recent conversation in which you felt affirmed and experienced a greater sense of well-being as a result. Which of Martin Seligman's five elements were in operation?

....

....

....

....

Can you recall being a part of a toxic conversation in which someone was diminished? Did you feel powerless to redirect it? Although unpleasant, did you learn something from it—such as how to see it coming in the future and ideas on how to redirect it?

....

....

....

....

....

....

CONSIDER

Which statement most reflects your current thoughts about this belief (conversations should be life-giving)?

○ I DISAGREE   ○ I'M SKEPTICAL   ○ I'M NOT SURE   ○ IT IS HELPFUL   ○ IT IS ESSENTIAL

On a scale of 1-10, how important is it for you to get better at facilitating conversations that are life-giving?

UNIMPORTANT ○─○─○─○─○─○─○─○─○ CRITICAL
                1 2 3 4 5 6 7 8 9 10

REMINDER:
Beliefs are complex. Your perspective may not align with this belief 100%. It is more important that you are honest with yourself and thoughtfully consider what your perspective is.

REFLECTIONS

Life-giving conversations are engaging, and it is very engaging to be encouraged. Consider the quote from Swami Vivikananda at the beginning of this chapter. How could you encourage your conversation partners? How can you encourage the highest ideal they hold? How does encouragement display respect, presence, and a genuine sense that we believe others count as much as we do?

....
....
....
....
....
....
....
....
....
....
....
....

Most often, a life-giving conversation increases our energy. Think about some ways you encourage another person, help yourself and your partner arrive at a better understanding of the things that really matter, and how to convey belief in one another. If a conversation is painful, what are some ways you could make sure that although the subtext of the conversation is difficult, you both walk away feeling encouraged, energized, and hopeful?

....
....
....
....
....
....
....
....
....
....
....
....
....
....
....

How can you be intentional about helping others experience Seligman's five elements of well-being as a result of your conversation? How can we leave others with positive emotion, a sense of having been engaged in something good, a feeling that they are in good standing in relationship with ourselves, that the conversation meant something and wasn't just a waste of time, and that something good was accomplished or achieved?

....
....
....
....
....
....
....
....
....
....
....

Anne Frank wrote that, "Everyone has inside them a piece of good news. The good news is you don't know how great you can be. How much you can love! What you can accomplish! And what your potential is." Consider that in a life-giving conversation, you use your words to reflect back to your partner the "good news" that is within them. Think about ways to reflect "good news" to someone. This is a great way to be more engaging, energizing, and affirming of another's identity.

....
....
....
....
....
....
....
....
....
....
....
....
....
....
....
....

LOOKING AT MY BELIEFS:

Conversation should be life-giving.

To understand how it might look and feel to honor or violate the belief that conversations should be life-giving, the following examples of top-down communication and partnership communication are provided. Use this simple scale to help you gauge the alignment you currently possess between your beliefs and your behavior (authenticity). The higher total score, the more oriented you are toward partnership communication. The lower total score, the more oriented you are toward top-down communication.

TOP-DOWN PRACTICES		**PARTNERSHIP PRACTICES**
Typically during conversations I'm not that engaged.	1 2 3 4 5 6 7 8 9 10	Typically during conversations I'm very engaged.
Most of my conversations take a lot out of me.	1 2 3 4 5 6 7 8 9 10	Most of my conversations energize me.
Usually I feel worse after having a conversation.	1 2 3 4 5 6 7 8 9 10	Usually I feel better after having a conversation.

Total Score ☐

What surprises you? What pleases you? Are you where you would like to be? What would you like to change?

....
....
....
....
....
....
....
....

Part 2

HABITS

The 10 Habits of
Better Conversations
///////////////////.

I have chosen to describe the practices in this book as habits rather than strategies, tactics, or use some other word that describes what we do. Of course, within habits there are strategies. The habit of building emotional connection, for example, involves the strategy of being mindful of others' bids for connection. Still, I've chosen *habits* as my key term because I think the best way to imagine communication practices is as a collection of habits. We all have communication habits, some good and some bad, that operate too often beneath the level of our awareness. *Better Conversations*, is about helping us become aware of our ineffective communication habits so we can replace them with effective habits. This companion book is intended to help you coach yourself in the practice of these new habits until they become automatic. People can learn the Better Conversation Beliefs and Habits on their own, with a partner, a coach, a team, or an entire school or district.

Changing Our Beliefs and Habits Involves Two Kinds of Knowledge:

RECOMMENDED READING:
The Knowledge Creating Company: How Japanese Companies Create the Dynamics of Innovation
//////////////,
IKUJIRO NONAKA
HIROTAKA TAKEUCHI

1. EXPLICIT KNOWLEDGE
Explicit knowledge "can be transmitted across individuals formally and easily [since it] can be articulated in formal language including grammatical statements, mathematical expressions, specifications, manuals, and so forth" (Nonaka and Takeuchi, 1995, p. viii).

2. TACIT KNOWLEDGE
Tacit knowledge "is a more important kind of knowledge" (p. viii). Tacit knowledge "is personal knowledge embedded in individual experience and involves intangible factors such as personal belief, perspective, and the value system" (p. viii). —Nonaka and Takeuchi According to Nonaka and Takeuchi, as depicted in the following figure, organizational learning involves three stages: (a) becoming aware of our tacit current beliefs and habits (tacit knowledge), (b) taking in descriptions of better ways of communicating (explicit knowledge) and then (c) practicing those ideas until they become new beliefs and habits (tacit again).

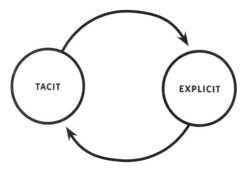

This book gives you the tools you need to move from tacit to explicit to tacit knowledge. It also includes the comments of others who employed this methodology to improve their communication skills.

10 Habits of Better Conversationalists:

1 Demonstrate Empathy
2 Listen
3 Foster Dialogue
4 Ask Better Questions
5 Make Emotional Connections
6 Be a Witness to the Good
7 Find Common Ground
8 Control Toxic Emotions
9 Redirect Toxic Conversations
10 Build Trust

DEMONSTRATE EMPATHY.

1

"Empathy is the very means by which we create social life and advance civilization."

////////////.

JEREMY RIFKIN

So much of communication, whether we are presenting to a large audience or consoling a three-year-old, depends on our ability to understand what our conversation partners think and feel. Before we design a beautiful slide or ask a probing question, our first thought should be, "What are my conversation partners thinking and feeling about this topic?"

Demonstrating empathy, despite its importance, is not very highly valued in our world today. People want to be shown empathy, but they're not terribly committed to showing it to others. Too often, we reduce other people to stereo-types or categories, and those stereotypes make it difficult for us to demonstrate empathy. People break into factions and label whole groups of people based on politics, gender, race, religion, sports preferences, or even the type of smart-phones they use. When we reduce people to types, we stop seeing them as fully human individuals.

Three Types of Empathy:

1. Empathy Toward Self
2. Affective Empathy
3. Cognitive Empathy

EMPATHY TOWARD SELF

My dad used to say that we are only as hard on others as we are on ourselves. Consider if you need to begin gentling your inner monologue. What if being gentler with yourself really could allow you to feel more empathy toward other people?

....
....
....
....
....
....

When people are hurting, they tend to hurt others. Because you want to be a person who doesn't add more hurt to an already aching world, it's important to understand your own pain and fear (to show yourself empathy) so you can understand how you may have been unconsciously bringing harm into your environment. What we don't know really can hurt us—and others. How can you move toward awareness of the way your own pain could cause you to injure others?

....
....
....
....
....
....

AFFECTIVE EMPATHY

Human persons need to be seen and to have a place. That is, when we share or mirror another person's emotions, we are engaging in affective empathy, which is to say that we provide place inside our hearts for the other person for a time. Sometimes it takes more time and energy than we have to see people where they are and accept that. Sometimes it takes courage to share another person's emotions. Like the guy who was doing his email while talking on the phone to his friend who'd lost her sister to cancer, we have good intentions to reach out, but we sometimes fall short in our follow-through. Since mastering follow-through could change the course of your relationship with your student, co-worker, administrator, or some other significant person in your life, think for a moment about the things that may stand in the way of you being able to be present, mirror the other person's emotions, and so provide a space for them within your heart for a while.

Consider the statement: "We struggle to listen with empathy because our ways of making sense of events can interfere with our ability to see the world as it is." Why might you be hesitant to offer empathy? What are those "fleeting questions of fear" (Bohm) that might hint that the world as it really is may be quite different from they way you've been allowing yourself to interpret it in the absence of empathic listening?

....
....
....
....
....
....

What are some "clever stories" you have told yourself (and maybe others) about people or events that have prevented you from being able to offer empathy?

"If we could read the secret history of our enemies, we should find in each man's suffering enough to disarm all hostility."
//////////////,
HENRY WADSWORTH LONGFELLOW

....
....
....
....
....
....

Is there some instance or challenge in which you've convinced yourself you're helpless? This is a clever story you tell yourself about yourself, and it flies in the face of having a growth mindset. Consider what the story might be. Nature hates a vacuum, so it's not enough to just stop telling yourself the clever story. How can you strengthen yourself—and open yourself to empathy—by adopting a growth mindset in place of the clever story?

....
....
....
....
....
....
....
....
....

COGNITIVE EMPATHY

Krznaric explains the difference between showing sympathy (an emotional response not shared) and offering empathy (sharing emotional response). While it seems impossible to share emotion that is grounded in someone else, this is where employing the imagination comes to your aid. You can take the imaginative leap (cognitive) that can help you see and feel what it must be like to go through what has hurt your conversation partner. That is how to share emotion, and show others you see them and they've a place, even for a few moments, in your heart. What does it look like as you practice sharing in someone else's emotion?

....

....

....

....

....

....

There are times when others' emotions are profoundly negative and upsetting. How can you understand what it might feel like to be them without getting sucked into a toxic, emotional vortex? It is a paradox to maintain a healthy emotional distance while sharing emotion with another person. How can this be worked out?

....

....

....

....

....

....

Consider Marshall B. Rosenberg's list of needs from *Non-Violent Communication* (autonomy, celebration, integrity, interdependence, spiritual communion, physical nurturance). Begin with self-empathy: what do you need? Now move to empathy for others. Begin to identify what it is that your conversation partner may need.

....

....

....

....

....

....

....

....

....

ACTIVITY 1

Think of a time when someone demonstrated true empathy toward you. What difference did that make to you?

ACTIVITY 2

1. Identify a person you'd like to understand better.
2. With your study group, talk about what you think that person's life might be like.
3. Write a one-minute, first-person description of what your person experiences.
4. Share that description with your group.

REFLECTIONS

LOOKING BACK:

 # Demonstrate Empathy

//

Use this form to look back on a conversation where you attempted to demonstrate empathy. Try to identify what you did well, where you could improve, and what you should do differently during future conversations.

What assumptions or preconceptions (if any) did you bring to the conversation that made it difficult to listen with empathy?

....

....

....

....

In what way did your self-interest, opinions, judgments, or fears interfere with your ability to listen with empathy?

....

....

....

....

How well did you recognize the emotions your conversation partner was feeling?

....

....

....

....

How well did you perceive the spoken and unspoken needs your conversation partner had?

....

....

....

....

What should you do differently in the future to be more effective at demonstrating empathy?

....

....

....

....

Demonstrate Empathy

///

Use this form to identify and note your comments about all the interactions you have with other people when you have stereotypical responses, yet you use your imagination to have more empathic responses. Use the spaces below to record your stereotypical response, your revised empathic response, and what you learned about yourself and others by choosing to see others with empathy.

1. Stereotypical Response

....
....
....

Empathic Response

....
....
....

2. Stereotypical Response

....
....
....

Empathic Response

....
....
....

3. Stereotypical Response

....
....
....

Empathic Response

....
....
....

What I Learned

....
....
....

Demonstrate Empathy

Use this form to prepare yourself for a conversation you are soon going to have where you intend to demonstrate empathy. Do your best to consider fully how you are thinking and feeling about the conversation, and how your conversation partner is thinking and feeling.

What assumptions or preconceptions are you bringing to the conversation that might make it difficult to listen with empathy?

....
....
....
....
....

What emotions do you anticipate your conversation partner might be feeling?

....
....
....
....
....

What needs do you think your conversation partner currently has regarding your future topic of conversation?

....
....
....
....
....

What other thoughts do you have about understanding your conversation partner's perspective and emotions?

....
....
....
....
....
....
....
....

LISTEN.

HABIT

////////////////////

2

"If there's no empathy, there's no listening. You can be hearing things, but I don't think you can be listening unless you have empathy."

////////////

CAROL WALKER

Next to having empathy for another person, becoming a good listener is paramount for effective communication. It is essential, and few would argue this point. And yet, when people begin to watch themselves in coaching videos, what usually strikes them is how they need to become better listeners.

So what do good listeners do? In part, good listening should be the natural outgrowth of the better conversation beliefs that we've just learned in section 1. If we see our conversation partners as equal partners, then conversation should be back and forth. If we truly want to hear what the other person has to say, then we should listen better.

4 Strategies for Being a Better Listener

1. COMMIT TO LISTEN.

(a) Consider the statement, "When we commit to listening, we enter conversations determined to let the other person speak." What does it look like when you practice that commitment in conversation?

....

....

....

....

....

(b) If one of the greatest challenges to listening is simply failing to recognize when you are not listening, would you be willing to video record a conversation and begin to coach yourself to be a better listener? With whom could you do this? When could you start?

....

....

....

....

....

(c) Do you agree that listening is something you can feel as much as see? What is an example of when you are able to feel authentic listening?

....

....

....

....

....

2. MAKE SURE YOUR PARTNER IS THE SPEAKER.

A great conversationalist lets the other person have the floor. What are some ways you can encourage your partner to be the speaker? What can you do when your partner doesn't want to be the speaker? Could years of not being listened to have trained her to be uncomfortable with her own voice? How can you encourage her?

....

....

....

....

....

....

3. PAUSE BEFORE YOU SPEAK AND ASK, "WILL MY COMMENT OPEN UP OR CLOSE DOWN THIS CONVERSATION?"

In order to be a good listener, you need to be at peace with silence instead of trying to fill it with knee-jerk verbiage. Do you need to cultivate an acceptance of quiet?

....

....

....

....

....

....

....

....

Sometimes when we are dealing with a surprising or shocking situation, or when we are confused, we are tempted to deal with anxiety by using unnecessary chatter. How can you deal with these instances in quieter, more mindful ways?

....

....

....

....

....

....

....

....

4. DON'T INTERRUPT.

What sorts of things fill you with a sense of urgency that tempts you to mindlessly interrupt others? What might you do to quell the urgency and diffuse the anxiety that accompanies it in order to fully attend to your conversation partner?

....

....

....

....

....

....

....

....

....

"The problem is this. You are taught what to say and how to sit, but the heart of good listening is authenticity. People "read" not only words and posture, but what's going on inside you. If your "stance" isn't genuine, the words won't matter ... If your intentions are false, no amount of careful wording or good posture will help. If your intentions are good, even clumsy language won't hinder you. Listening is only powerful and effective if it is authentic. Authenticity means that you are listening because you are curious and because you care, not just because you are supposed to. The issue, then, is this: Are you curious? Do you care?"

//////////////

DOUGLAS STONE

BRUCE PATTON

SHEILA HEEN

A Level One listener is someone who has disciplined herself to let another person speak without interrupting. A Level Two listener not only allows space for another person to speak, but is able to empathically offer another person a place inside her heart for a time in order to better understand the person's emotions. Would you rate yourself as a Level One or Level Two listener? Are you where you'd like to be as a listener?

....
....
....
....
....
....
....
....
....
....
....

REFLECTIONS

....
....
....
....
....
....
....
....
....
....
....
....
....
....
....
....
....
....
....

Listen

Complete this form after you have recorded a conversation in which you tried to use the listening strategies. You can complete it while watching or after watching the conversation.

On a scale of 1-10, how interested were you in what the other person had to say?

Not Interested ◯─◯─◯─◯─◯─◯─◯─◯─◯─◯ Very Interested
                1 2 3 4 5 6 7 8 9 10

Is there anything you can do differently next time to be more interested in what your conversation partner has to say?

....

....

....

How many minutes were you the speaker or listener?

SPEAKER	LISTENER

Is there anything you can do differently next time to listen more?

....

....

....

What did you do that opened up or closed down the conversation?

....

....

....

Is there anything you can do differently next time to encourage your conversation partner to open up?

....

....

....

What else could you try to do differently next time to improve as a listener?

....

....

....

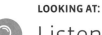

Listen

What conversation did you observe to identify how people listen?

....

....

What was the topic of the conversation?

....

....

On a scale of 1-10, how well did people listen to each other?

Poor ⓞ—ⓞ—ⓞ—ⓞ—ⓞ—ⓞ—ⓞ—ⓞ—ⓞ—ⓞ Excellent
       1 2 3 4 5 6 7 8 9 10

What strategies or habits did you see people use that showed they appeared to be listening?

....

....

How did people react when they were heard?

....

....

What habits did you see people use that showed they appeared to not be listening?

....

....

How did people react when they were not heard?

....

....

What did you learn about how you should listen to other people?

....

....

....

....

Listen

///

What is a conversation where you intend to practice listening with empathy?

....

....

....

On a scale of 1 – 10, how interested do you expect to be in this conversation?

Poor O–O–O–O–O–O–O–O–O–O Excellent
         1 2 3 4 5 6 7 8 9 10

On a scale of 1 – 10, how committed are you to listening with empathy?

Poor O–O–O–O–O–O–O–O–O–O Excellent
         1 2 3 4 5 6 7 8 9 10

What can you do to increase your interest and commitment?

....

....

....

What can you do to ensure that the focus of the conversation is on others rather than yourself?

....

....

....

Have you cleared your mind? Is there anything else you need to do to make sure you are ready to listen without preconceptions and with empathy?

....

....

....

What can you do to make sure you focus on the emotions and needs of others?

....

....

....

....

....

FOSTER DIALOGUE.

3

*"[When we embrace dialogue],
collectively, we can be more
insightful, more intelligent
than we can possibly be
individually."*

//////////////////

PETER SENGE

One of the ways Better Conversationalists align their actions with their beliefs that conversation partners should have autonomy, be heard, and that conversation should be a back-and-forth, life-giving experience is to begin to cultivate the habit of fostering dialogue. Dialogical conversations almost always lead to better outcomes and promote greater learning because dialogue begins with strength and dignity and an intentional focus on others. It does away with top-down, passive power struggles where conversations are merely endured and then forgotten as quickly as possible. Participants in a dialogue all practice listening with empathy and respect for the other person's views. A dialogical conversation is led by voices determined to keep the conversation open rather than closed. Far from being impossible or a rare occurrence, dialogical conversations can become one of our personal, conversational norms as we begin to practice incorporating this habit.

Freire's Conditions for Dialogue

- » Humility
- » Hope
- » Faith
- » Critical Thinking
- » Love

Practical Reasons for Fostering Dialogue

The old saying goes that two heads are better than one. Dialogue harnesses the power and creativity of everyone's minds. What keeps people from being willing to tap into such an amazing resource? What is more important: to be the expert at the table or to open up conversation so greater learning and better outcomes can be had?

William Isaacs provides the following question to help recognize if the conversation we are having is a dialogue or not. Are you experiencing energy, possibility, and safety in your conversations?

Moral Reasons to Foster Dialogue

TOP-DOWN COMMUNICATION IS DEHUMANIZING

The problem with top-down communication is that it forces people to live in extremes: I'm extremely right, you're extremely wrong; I'm the expert, you're not; I have a right to speak, you don't. It's dehumanizing on every side because both winners and losers are isolated. Dialogue is about navigating to the *via media*, the humanizing middle ground where all are welcome, free to think and speak, and are respected. What can you do right now to gauge where you are on the line of extremes, and, if needed, how can you move to a more central position where dialogue is the norm?

....
....
....
....
....

ASSUMPTIONS PREVENT US FROM SEEING OTHERS AS WHO THEY REALLY ARE

Bohm explains that dialogue is difficult because of assumptions we hold about the basic stuff of life (the meaning of life, politics, religion, etc.). Jot down some assumptions you hold and rise to immediately defend. Now think about what it might look like to foster dialogue in the face of those deeply held assumptions.

....
....
....
....
....
....

STRATEGIES TO MOVE BEYOND ASSUMPTIONS

1. Consider Others' Thoughts and Feelings
2. Clarify the Meaning of Words and Concepts
3. Provide Contextual Information
4. Identify your Own False Assumptions
5. Use Stories and Analogies

....
....
....
....
....
....

Most adults probably aren't going to switch their views on religion or politics, but it is necessary to imagine how you can have dialogue (where people are free to honestly and respectfully speak) despite assumptions. Is it important for you to continue to gain awareness of your assumptions and become a facilitator of dialogue?

....
....
....
....
....

Given that everyone questions everything at some point in time—and they're free to do so as people with their own minds—what would it look and feel like to feel less threatened in a dialogue where others have assumptions different than your own? What do you imagine an honest, yet gracious dialogue would sound like? Are you willing to be as gracious with others and their assumptions as you hope they'll be with you and yours? Are you as willing to let go of your false assumptions as you hope others will be to let go of theirs?

....

....

....

....

....

....

Letting go of assumptions that are false is one of the most difficult things to do. Consider that reality for a moment. Think about how hard it is for you. Now give that same allowance to another person. This is important work, but it is not easy work. Thought difficult, creating a more equitable and respectful environment is a worthy struggle.

....

....

....

....

....

....

How can using the strategies of considering others' thoughts and feelings, clarifying the meaning of words and concepts, providing contextual information, identifying your own false assumptions, and using stories and analogies help you move beyond assumption roadblocks to dialogue?

....

....

....

....

....

....

....

Strategies to Foster Dialogue by Balancing Advocacy and Inquiry

In a dialogue, it is important that everyone speaks. One of the most practical things to gauge is who is doing all the talking. We all know that one person who calls us up and talks non-stop for an hour, and all we have to do is say, "Hmm ... mmm-hmmm. Wow."

This is not a dialogue. It is an anti-dialogical nightmare that the kindest endure and the thoughtless foist upon anyone who is willing to put up with it. Sometimes people say about somebody, "Oh, he's a talker ..." as a nice way of warning, "You're not going to get a word in edge-wise, and you're going to be really, really late for your next appointment." It's not just that the person doesn't listen; he never stops talking. Are you a "talker"? Or are you a person who has learned how to balance advocacy (your own voice) with inquiry (actively seeking to discover more about the other person's perspective)?

BE HUMBLE.
Consider the idea of seeing conversations as a testing ground for your ideas—where you embrace the fact that you don't really know all there is to know about something. What does that look like?

....

....

....

....

....

LISTEN WITH EMPATHY.
What gesture of empathy can you offer to the other person? A helpful action? An understanding comment? A genuine apology?

....

....

....

....

....

OPEN YOURSELF TO NEW IDEAS.
What does it look like for you to enter into a conversation with the desire to find out if you are wrong? This is not an easy question to answer, so give yourself some time to think this through.

....

....

....

....

SURFACE AND SUSPEND ASSUMPTIONS.

Knowledge is power, and some of the most important knowledge we need to surface is knowledge about how our assumptions and opinions came to be our own. William Isaacs invites us to "relax our grip on certainty ..." Use the following Root Cause Analysis form to figure out how you came to hold a particular assumption. Is it necessary for you to still hold this position? Is it something that you can release?

....

....

....

....

....

....

....

....

Root Cause Analysis

Use this Root Cause Analysis form to examine how you came to hold certain assumptions or beliefs. Use what you learn to determine if you need to continue to hold this assumption or belief.

Why or how did I come to believe or assume that:

....

....

....

Why or how did I come to believe or assume that?

....

....

....

Why or how did I come to believe or assume that?

....

....

....

Why or how did I come to believe or assume that?

....

....

....

Why or how did I come to believe or assume that?

....

....

....

Why or how did I come to believe or assume that?

....

....

....

Consider the statement, "To balance advocacy with inquiry, we need to suspend our assumptions. This doesn't mean we give up our opinions; it just means we don't make the point of conversation our own point." Do you find this helpful?

....

....

....

....

....

QUESTIONS THAT ENCOURAGE DIALOGUE

» What do you think the _____ suggests?

» What leads you to believe_____?

» What are some other ways we can look at that?

» What are we uncertain about?

» What is your hope for _____?

» What if nothing happens?

....

....

....

....

....

EXAMPLES OF A THIRD SIDE

////////////////

1. Video

2. Data

3. Forms (such as Better Conversations reflection forms)

4. Questioning Routines

Dialogue Structures

Dialogue structures are ways of organizing how people interact so they will likely engage in dialogue.

» Brainstorming

» Affinity Diagrams

» Nominal Group Technique

» deBono's Six Thinking Hats

» Owen's Open Space

BRAINSTORMING

Brainstorming is a dialogue structure familiar to most. First described by Alex Faickney Osborn in his book *Applied Imagination* (1953), brainstorming is a simple process where a group of people lists ideas or thoughts about a particular topic. Brainstorming is a free activity, but two rules are basic to effective brainstorming: (a) Focus on quantity: During brainstorming, a group should try to come up with as may ideas as possible, the more ideas the better; (b) Withhold criticism so that people feel free to generate more ideas, and more innovative suggestions. If participants aren't worried about how good or bad an idea is, they will be more likely to make suggestions. Evaluation of the ideas can occur after every idea has been listed.

AFFINITY DIAGRAMS

The idea of brainstorming was adapted by Japanese anthropologist Jiro Kawakita, who created affinity diagrams. Affinity diagrams are frequently used in collaborative group activities. The affinity diagram process involves three steps. First, all participants pick a topic to be discussed and write down their ideas on sticky notes. Second, they affix all their post-it notes to the white board or a wall in the room where they are meeting. Then, usually without talking, they sort the sticky into groups that are related. Affinity diagrams allow a large amount of information to be generated and organized very quickly.

NOMINAL GROUP TECHNIQUE

Nominal (in name only) group process involves groups of four to six. Everyone involved will be working on a written statement of the problem to be addressed. Each person spends about five minutes writing out his or her ideas about or responses to the problem. Once everyone has done this, small groups are formed and each member contributes one idea to be put on the chalkboard or chart tablet. The process continues around the group until all the ideas are on the chart. No ideas are eliminated at this point, but clarification may be asked for. If there are time constraints, the whole process can take place in a group setting, going round robin. Participants then rank their top three choices and the facilitator circles the ideas with the most votes.

EDWARD DE BONO'S SIX THINKING HATS

de Bono's *Six Thinking Hats* (1985) expands the traditional idea of a devil's advocate or court jester; that is, a person whose role is to point out alternative viewpoints with respect to whatever is being discussed. deBono suggests six different perspectives, defined as different thinking hats, which represent different perspectives people can take during discussions. DeBono's six hats are: (a) white hat, focussed on data, empirical evidence, and facts; (b) red hat, focused on emotions, intuition, and gut responses; (c) black hat, focused on identifying what could go wrong with a plan; (d) yellow hat, focused on all that is good about a topic of discussion; (f) green hat, focused on creatively exploring a variety of options related to whatever is being discussed; and (g) blue hat, focused on managing the process of the conversation itself.

HARRISON OWEN'S OPEN SPACE TECHNOLOGY
Harrison Owen's *Open Space Technology* (1997) describes a group conversation process that is driven entirely by the interests and choices of participants. During open space, participants list topics they would like to discuss and then organize themselves by joining with others who are interested in the identified topics. Whoever proposes a topic that is discussed serves as a host for the conversation and generally keeps the conversation moving. If people don't feel they are contributing to or learning from a group, they move to another group. Owen calls this the Law of Two Feet, suggesting that if a conversation isn't working, you use your feet to find another one.

Foster Dialogue

///

Use this form to analyze a conversation where assumptions seemed to get in the way of meaningful dialogue. List the topics that were discussed in the center column. List your assumptions on the right side of the page under the "My Assumptions" column. List what you believe your partner's assumptions were on the left side of the page under "Others' Assumptions."

OTHERS' ASSUMPTIONS	TOPICS DISCUSSED	MY ASSUMPTIONS

REFLECTIONS

LOOKING AT:

Foster Dialogue (1 of 2)

Complete this form after you have recorded a conversation in which you tried to engage in dialogue. You can complete it while watching or after watching the conversation.

Put a mark on the line to indicate who did most of the talking in this conversation:

Me   **My Partner**

100%   50/50%   100%

Is there anything you can do to ensure both partners contribute equally to the conversation next time?

....

....

....

Put a mark on the line below to indicate what percentage of the time you were talking in this conversation:

Me   **My Partner**

100%   50/50%   100%

Is there anything you should do next time to enable your partner to speak more?

....

....

....

Put a mark on the line that indicates how much of the time you were telling your opinion in the conversation:

                            Listening, questioning, or
Telling my opinion   **mutually exploring**

100%   50/50%   100%

Is there anything you should do next time to change the way you ask questions?

....

....

....

Foster Dialogue (2 of 2)

Put a mark on the line that indicates to what extent the outcome of the conversation was one that you proposed, your partner proposed, or was mutually constructed:

Me   **Mutual**   **My Partner**

├──┼──┼──┼──┼──┼──┼──┼──┼──┤

100%   50/50%   100%

Is there anything else you can do to make your next conversation more of a dialogue?

....

....

....

....

....

....

....

....

....

Foster Dialogue

//

Identify a future conversation and use this form to help you gain insights that will help you foster dialogue.

What is your opinion?

....

....

What are your conversation partner's needs?

....

....

....

What words do you need to define with your partner?

....

....

....

What contextual information does your partner need to understand what you are talking about?

....

....

....

What stories or analogies can you use to make this conversation clearer?

....

....

....

Are you willing to:

- ○ not have your opinion accepted?
- ○ admit you're wrong?
- ○ listen most of the time—giving everyone equal opportunity to talk?
- ○ look for disconfirming evidence?
- ○ suspend your assumptions?
- ○ identify a devil's advocate?

What else can you do to encourage dialogue?

....

....

....

ASK BETTER QUESTIONS.

HABIT

////////////////////

4

"A good question is like a lever used to pry open the stuck lid on a paint can."

////////////

FRANCES PEAVEY

Good questions open up conversations, generate respect, accelerate learning, and build relationships. Questions are the yang to complete the yin of listening, the balance to advocacy. If we don't ask questions, we won't have the opportunity to listen. If we don't listen, our questions won't serve much purpose. When we see others as equals, we usually give them at least equal time at the center of our conversation, and that requires asking questions that allow our conversation partners to say what they wish. By asking good questions, we demonstrate what Tony Stoltzfus in *Coaching Questions* calls "conversational generosity." By learning to ask smarter, better questions, we learn far more about the other person, and the conversations we are able to have become better in nearly every way.

Strategies to Ask Better Questions

- » Be Curious
- » Avoid Unhelpful Questions
- » Ask Open, Opinion Questions
- » Be Mindful of Closed, Right/Wrong Questions
- » Be Nonjudgmental

BE CURIOUS

If, as Edgar Schein has said, asking questions is a powerful way to show interest, generate curiosity, concern, and clarify general statements, can you see how asking questions can be an exciting and enjoyable conversational strategy?

....

....

....

....

How do you feel when people show an interest in you?

....

....

....

....

....

AVOID UNHELPFUL QUESTIONS

Jon Farrell-Higgins describes four types of unhelpful questions: demand questions, set-up questions, stump questions, and angry questions. How could each of these questions be seen as thinly disguised attempts to manipulate and demean another person?

....

....

....

....

....

OPEN, OPINION QUESTIONS

What are examples of times when these types of questions are particularly helpful?

....

....

....

....

....

BE MINDFUL OF CLOSED, RIGHT/WRONG QUESTIONS

How effective are these types of questions for dialogue? When might you need to use a closed-ended question?

....

....

....

....

....

....

How can you use skillful questions to place a premium on student voice? How important is the voice of the student to you? How can you use questions to honor students' humanity and unlock students' growth?

....

....

....

....

....

....

Think of a current challenge you are facing as an individual or as a team (Planning? Coaching? Teaching?). Use Berger's "Why, What If, and How" questioning framework to come to new insights.

....

....

....

....

....

....

BE NONJUDGMENTAL

How important is it to provide a psychologically safe environment in which questions are asked? How does judgment create an unsafe environment? If needed, refer back to Belief 4 to review the importance of maintaining a nonjudgmental atmosphere.

....

....

....

....

....

....

Ask Better Questions

///

Audio or video record a conversation. The conversation could be at work, home, or in the community, but pick an important one (for example, a goal-setting conversation, if you are a coach). Make sure your conversation partner is OK with you recording it. Afterwards, listen to your conversation and code your questions.

QUESTION	OPEN	CLOSED	OPINION	RIGHT/WRONG
	○	○	○	○
	○	○	○	○
	○	○	○	○
	○	○	○	○
	○	○	○	○
	○	○	○	○
	○	○	○	○
	○	○	○	○
	○	○	○	○
	○	○	○	○
	○	○	○	○
	○	○	○	○
	○	○	○	○
	○	○	○	○
	○	○	○	○
	○	○	○	○
	○	○	○	○
	○	○	○	○
	○	○	○	○

Ask Better Questions

//

Use this area to record effective questions you hear during day-to-day conversation. Effective questions usually provoke thought, dialogue, or foster better conversations in other ways. Effective questions are often open and opinion questions.

....
....
....
....
....
....
....
....
....
....
....
....
....
....
....
....
....

Use this area to record ineffective questions you hear during day-to-day conversation. Ineffective questions often have obvious answers, fail to provoke thought, and usually do not foster better conversations. Ineffective questions are often closed, right/wrong questions.

....
....
....
....
....
....
....
....
....
....
....
....
....
....

Ask Better Questions

//

Identify a future conversation where you will need to ask effective questions. Review the list of questions below to identify questions you might use to foster dialogue and share understanding. Put a checkmark beside any questions you might use in the identified conversation.

QUESTION

○ Given the time we have today, what is the most important thing you and I should be talking about? (Susan Scott)

○ What if nothing changes? So what? What are the implications for you and your students? (Susan Scott)

○ What is the ideal outcome? (Susan Scott)

○ What can we do to resolve this issue? (Susan Scott)

○ Tell me about what you felt.

○ Tell me a little about this...

○ What leads you to believe ....?

○ What went well? What surprised you? What did you learn? What will you do differently next time?

○ What do you think about ....?

○ On a scale of 1-10, how close are you to your ideal classroom? (Steve Barkley)

○ What are you seeing that shows the the strategy is successful? (Steve Barkley)

○ What impact would _____ have? (Steve Barkley)

○ When have you seen _____ ? (Steve Barkley)

○ What do you think the _____ suggests?

○ What are some other ways we can look at that?

○ What are we uncertain about?

○ What is your hope for _____ ?

○ What if nothing happens?

REFLECTIONS

MAKE EMOTIONAL CONNECTIONS.

5

"Complex, fulfilling relationships don't suddenly appear in our lives fully formed. Rather, they develop one encounter at a time."

///////////////

JOHN GOTTMAN

Connection is about strengthening our relationships by building emotional connections and being witnesses to the good. We can increase the emotional connection we feel with others if we are intentional about reaching out to connect with them. And, as John Gottman teaches, there are thousands of ways in which we can extend bids of connection to others. If we are mindful of how bids shape the emotional landscape of our schools, homes, and communities, we should find many opportunities to turn toward bids from others. To do this, we need to take the time to listen, observe, and interact. Taking the time to connect with others is just as important as taking the time to observe in the classroom. People long for connection, and emotionally intelligent leaders are constantly watching for opportunities to respond positively to others' bids for connection.

Strategies for Making Emotional Connections

» Understand and Use Gottman's Bids for Connection
» Be Fully Present
» Be Persistent
» Walk the Talk

What are some examples of bids for connection?

TURNING TOWARD

How have you accepted someone else's bid recently by turning toward?

TURNING AWAY

Have you turned away from someone's bid for connection?

TURNING AGAINST

Can you think of a time when you turned against a bid? If you haven't, have you watched someone else turn against a bid for connection?

....

....

....

....

....

....

ACTIVITY

Think of one person with whom you would like to be better connected. Now, think about some creative, professional ways to make bids for connection.

....

....

....

....

....

....

BE FULLY PRESENT

To be present is more than being in the same airspace as someone else. True presence means being attentive to the humanity of others and seeing that as the most important thing—not just the task at hand.

In order to respond to bids for connection, we have to first be aware of those bids. This requires being fully present to your conversation partner. What things typically distract you? How can you limit those distractions when you are in conversation with others?

In Zulu text, *sawu bona* means, "I see you." It isn't just seeing another person, but attending to his or her humanity.

How do you let people know that you see them?

What does it feel like when others see you and respond to your personhood in a generous way?

BE PERSISTENT

Sometimes people don't respond to bids because they aren't practiced in being present to others, or they're too distracted. Is it always personal if someone turns away from a bid, then? How can realizing that it's not necessary to take it personally encourage you to be persistent and keep reaching out?

There are many creative ways to offer others bids for connection. However, there are some legitimate reasons why people turn away from certain bids. For instance, somebody who struggles with any form of addiction may turn away from a bid that could put their sobriety in jeopardy. Some folks have religious beliefs that prohibit them from accepting certain types of bids. Part of being present to another person is to consider who they are, what they believe, and to honor the struggles he or she may have and then shape your bids in an appropriate fashion. When it seems that someone has turned away from a bid to connect, it may simply mean they need a different avenue of connection. The habits of being nonjudgmental and learning to ask better questions are helpful when you begin to practice making appropriate bids for connection.

WALK IT—DON'T JUST TALK IT.

Lots of people bandy about communication jargon, but sometimes their words aren't backed up by internal integrity and genuine action. As a student of Better Conversations, how can you guard against this tendency to "talk it" more than you "walk it"?

REFLECTIONS

Make Emotional Connections

Record yourself in a conversation. This could be personal or professional. Point the camera toward your conversation partner, as long as he or she agrees. Afterwards, watch the video carefully to see whether you or your partner (a) made bids, (b) turned toward, (c) turned away, or (d) turned against. Pay particular attention to nonverbal communication.

When did you see your partner make a bid, turn toward, away from, or against one of your bids?

....

....

....

....

....

When did you miss opportunities to makes bids to your partner or turn toward your partner's bids?

....

....

....

....

....

When did you see yourself or your partner turn away from or against a bid?

....

....

....

....

....

Make Emotional Connections
(1 of 2)

//

PEOPLE WATCHING

Take 30 minutes to watch people around you and observe how they (a) make bids, (b) turn toward, (c) turn away, or (d) turn against. Pay particular attention to nonverbal communication.

What examples of bids did you see?

....

....

....

How did you see people turn toward bids?

....

....

....

What did they do that opened up or closed down the conversation?

....

....

....

How did you see people turn away from bids?

....

....

....

How did you see people turn against bids?

....

....

....

🔍 # Make Emotional Connections
(2 of 2)

//

EMOTIONAL BIDS

Use this form to record the emotional bids you make each day. Use it whenever you want to remind yourself to make more bids. You only need to include a few words to record the bid, such as, "offered to get coffee for Alex." The purpose of the form is to prompt you to make numerous bids for emotional connection. Don't spend more than a few seconds noting each bid. You may want to carry this form with you and just write down what occurs. You can type your notes at a later date.

DATE	BID

Make Emotional Connections

///

Identify someone you think you especially need to connect with more effectively.

What can you do to make more bids?

....

....

....

....

....

What can you do to turn towards more effectively?

....

....

....

....

....

What can you do to be more mindful of people's need to connect?

....

....

....

....

....

What else can you do to build an emotional connection with your partner?

....

....

....

....

....

BE A WITNESS TO THE GOOD.

6

"Nearly every organization or work team we've spent time with ... astonishingly under-communicates the genuinely positive, appreciative, and admiring experiences of its members. This is ... a terrible deprivation of the vitality of a work setting."

//////////////

ROBERT KEGAN

LISA LAHEY

One of the most powerful ways to connect with others is to share our positive experiences of them. This type of validation is encouraging, inspiring, and profoundly pleasant. As business guru Tom Peters has commented, "The simple act of paying positive attention to people has a great deal to do with productivity." But being a witness to the good is not always easy. Most of us are quicker to notice the negative than the positive. If we have a better under-standing of how our attention works, we can get a better understanding of why being a witness to the good can be difficult and why it is so important to learn to do it effectively.

It can be difficult to be a witness to the good because there are two types of attention, and there are specific ways of giving attention that are far more effective than others.

Think about the difference between bottom-up vs. top-down attention (note this is probably the only time in this book that the words top-down have an entirely positive connotation).

BOTTOM-UP COMMUNICATION	TOP-DOWN COMMUNICATION

How to Develop a "Language of Ongoing Regard."

(Kegan and Lahey): Direct, specific, non-attributive comments

> *"Ongoing regard is not about praising, stroking, or positively defining a person to herself or to others. We say it again: it is about enhancing the quality of a special kind of information. It is about informing the person about our experiences of him or her."*
>
> //////////////
>
> **ROBERT KEGAN**
> **LISA LAHEY**

POSITIVE COMMENTS OFTEN FAIL BECAUSE THEY ARE:

1. Indirect
2. General
3. Attributive

DIRECT/SPECIFIC COMMENTS

Positive comments that are effective are comments spoken directly to the person the comments are about. Is it difficult for you to be direct? Are you a naturally shy person? If so, what can you do to begin to feel comfortable offering your positive comments directly to the other person?

....

....

....

....

....

....

Specific comments are the details of what we are praising; they're not general or attributive.

....

....

....

....

....

....

NONATTRIBUTIVE COMMENTS

These positive comments describe our experience of other people instead of verbally lobbing a vague attribute of theirs back at them (e.g., you're kind).

Think of someone you'd like to praise. What are the specific details of what they did that were praiseworthy? How can you share your experience of their actions instead of saying something vague like, "You're a great teacher."

....

....

....

....

....

....

How is being a witness to the good different from the dishonesty of self-serving flattery?

....
....
....
....
....
....

Flattery and affirmation aren't the same thing, but sometimes they are treated similarly. What are the differences between these two terms?

....
....
....
....
....
....
....
....

How does focusing on effort rather than intelligence when praising our children or students help develop within them a growth mind-set rather than a fixed mindset?

....
....
....
....
....
....
....
....
....
....
....
....
....
....
....
....

Be a Witness to the Good

//.

Record yourself in a conversation during which you share positive information. This could be a personal or professional conversation. Afterwards, watch the video to analyze how effectively you were a witness to the good.

Note the praise you gave your partner below and identify the attributes of your praise:

COMMENTS	ATTRIBUTIVE	NONATTRIBUTIVE	SPECIFIC	DIRECT	
	○	○	○	○	○
	○	○	○	○	○
	○	○	○	○	○
	○	○	○	○	○
	○	○	○	○	○
	○	○	○	○	○
	○	○	○	○	○
	○	○	○	○	○
	○	○	○	○	○
	○	○	○	○	○
	○	○	○	○	○

What should you do differently (if anything) to share positive information more effectively in the future?

....

....

....

....

....

....

Be a Witness to the Good

Describe a time when someone shared some positive feedback with you that had a positive impact on you.

....

....

....

....

....

What was it about that feedback that made it so effective?

....

....

....

....

....

What can you learn from that experience about how you can be a witness to the good?

....

....

....

....

....

Be a Witness to the Good

Use this form to prepare yourself for a conversation you are soon to have where you intend to be a witness to the good.

What general praise would you give to your partner?

_____

_____

_____

_____

_____

What evidence supports your positive observation?

_____

_____

_____

_____

_____

What can you do to make it more specific?

_____

_____

_____

_____

_____

FIND COMMON GROUND.

HABIT

////////////////////

7

"I note the obvious differences between each sort and type, but we are more alike, my friends, than we are unalike."

////////////////

MAYA ANGELOU

In our day-to-day experiences, we can easily lose sight of how much we hold in common with others, especially when people let us down, disagree with us, treat us poorly, or stand in the way of us achieving our goals. We can become frustrated when others' legitimate questions slow down a change initiative we are championing. However, if we label others as resistors just because they need time to think through new learning, we may make change more unlikely by damaging relationships.

One way to have better conversations is to notice and remember the similarities we share with others. When we find common ground, we will have healthy relationships and better conversations. Being intentional about finding common ground is an important part of effective communication.

The purpose of finding common ground is to improve relationships by identifying how we are similar to others. We do this by seeking out common denominators, avoiding common dividers, using language that unites rather than divides, and by learning how to recognize and avoid toxic connections.

....
....
....
....
....
....

When we begin to practice finding common ground with others, we realize that it can be very difficult to see our similarities with others. There are four common perceptual errors that make things harder:

1. Confirmation Bias
2. Habituation
3. Primacy Effect
4. Stereotypes

CONFIRMATION BIAS

How have you tended to seek out information that supports your own assumptions? How often do you find yourself "preaching to the choir"? Recently, a famous pop singer lost her battle with drugs. She had many people around her who should have seen her fatal descent into addiction. It became clear that while those people cared about her, they were on her payroll, and their main jobs were to make things happen that she wanted to happen with no regard for her health. In other words, they were her "yes men" instead of people who could have honest conversations with her and hold her accountable. Do you prefer to surround yourself with yes men? Or do you welcome, however uncomfortably, people who will tell you what you need to hear rather than what you want to hear? Is there a particular person you trust who could be your accountability partner?

....
....
....
....
....
....
....
....

HABITUATION

Habituation is a curse. The people or things that once delighted us become passé and boring. It is a discipline to cultivate the gratefulness that is habituation's antidote. What people—and what behaviors and characteristics within those people—are you grateful for today? How can grateful attentiveness help you keep sight of all the things you hold in common with others?

....
....
....
....
....
....
....

PRIMACY EFFECT

How does it feel when you realize that with some people you can do no wrong, whereas with others, no matter what you do, you just can't please them? How does understanding primacy effect help you understand how this happens?

....
....
....
....
....
....
....
....

Are there any ways in which you have fallen prey to the primacy effect with others?

....
....
....
....
....
....
....
....
....
....
....
....

Think of a person you met who made a positive first impression on you. Think about someone you met who made a negative first impression. Compare what the course of your relationship has been like with each person.

....

....

....

....

....

....

....

When we understand the primacy effect, we are able to relax and understand how people can seem to never be happy with us. They probably aren't even conscious of the perceptual error that keeps them from seeing all the good we bring to the table. This knowledge of the primacy effect helps us to be understanding of others.

....

....

....

....

....

....

....

....

STEREOTYPES

It's surprising to think that stereotypes can be positive in nature. We are more familiar with negative stereotyping. The heart of the stereotype is that we flatten the unique personhood of others. The pressure someone feels to perform under a positive stereotype is just as destructive as the heartbreaking diminishing of the negative stereotype. How can you work to see past a type and see to the person in front of you? Have you been stereotyped? What does it feel like?

....

....

....

....

....

....

....

....

Strategies for Finding Common Ground

1. Seek Common Denominators by Using ICARE
2. Avoid Common Dividers
3. Use Words That Unite; Avoid Words That Divide
4. Avoid Toxic Connections

In order to work past perceptual errors once we are aware of them, we need strategies to help us continue finding common ground. Those strategies include seeking common denominators (ICARE), avoiding common dividers, using language that unites rather than divides, and avoiding toxic connections. When we commit and plan to look for common ground, we typically find it.

Seek Common Denominators

INTERESTS
What interests do you share with others?

CONVICTIONS
What common convictions do you hold?

ACTIVITIES
What types of common activities connect you to others?

ROLES
It is fun to talk about the challenges and rewards of common roles. If you share a role with someone, try asking them what they find most delightful and most challenging about that role.

EXPERIENCES
There are as many experiences to share as there are people.

Keep in mind that professionalism should be honored when considering different avenues of connection. Some experiences are simply not appropriate to talk about in a work environment, and doing so may ruin your chances to connect with key people. We need to be wise and professional when we connect with others.

Avoid Common Dividers

Every strength has a flip-side weakness. And so it is with the potential common denominators listed above (ICARE). Consider how each of these things has historically been divisive. When it becomes obvious that a potential common denominator is something that will be divisive, how can you navigate through that and find another way to seek common ground? When a situation like this presents itself, we have to be especially intentional about seeking common ground. What might that look like?

Recall Abraham Lincoln's words: "We are not enemies, but friends. We must not be enemies. Though passion may have strained, it must not break our bonds of affection."

....

....

....

....

....

....

....

Use Words That Unite; Avoid Words That Divide

When we communicate, we are building something real, yet intangible with our words. How can we use words to build unity? What words would help you build unity with a person you're struggling to find common ground with right now?

....

....

....

....

....

....

....

....

....

....

....

....

....

....

....

While there are obvious words and phrases that divide people, a rule of thumb to keep in mind when trying to avoid using divisive language is to only say things that put others in the most complimentary light. Jennifer's dear friend, Melissa, once told her, "I always try to find one thing that is good about a person, and I focus on that." It's hard to be divisive when watching for the good and beautiful within people.

What is one excellent thing about a person you are having a difficult time finding common ground with? When we anchor our perceptions of others on at least one good thing, it's much easier to move toward unity.

Avoid Toxic Connections

Recall this statement: "Unhealthy or toxic connection involves any kind of common ground that diminishes others."

Gossiping, nagging, whining, and complaining are all forms of toxic communication around which people often connect. Why are these toxic connections so easily tolerated? Ask yourself if this is the kind of connection you want undergirding your environment.

Take the above statement further and consider that people often connect with others by diminishing people who don't have anything to do with work. Are your words and actions diminishing to another person, present or not? Are you connecting with someone in a way that is diminishing to someone else?

....
....
....
....
....
....
....
....

Take note that connections based on diminishing another are not only unhealthy, but are also unstable and are often highly destructive. Imagine ways to connect with people that do not diminish anyone else.

....
....
....
....
....
....
....
....
....
....
....
....
....
....
....
....
....
....
....
....
....
....
....
....

REFLECTIONS

Find Common Ground

//

Use this form to look at a conversation where you either did or did not find common ground.

Briefly describe the conversation you experienced.

....

....

....

....

....

What common denominators did you find between you and your conversation partner?

....

....

....

....

....

Please note any words that you or your conversation partner said that created unity or division during the conversation.

....

....

....

....

....

Did you do anything to avoid common dividers?

....

....

....

....

....

Is there anything you should do differently to be more effective at finding common ground?

....

....

....

....

....

Find Common Ground (1 of 2)

//

REGISTER

Keep track for a day of interactions when you seek out common ground. What was the interaction? What did you do? What was the outcome?

INTERACTION	WHAT DID YOU DO?	OUTCOME

Find Common Ground (2 of 2)

//

WITH A PARTNER

Use this form to explore Finding Common Ground and to try out the ICARE model. Simply use the questions to identify what common ground you hold with your conversation partner.

Interests: What are your interests or passions (books, food, restaurants, music, sports teams, travel, and so on)?

....

....

....

....

Convictions: What are your important intellectual, political, artistic, social action, or religious beliefs?

....

....

....

....

Activities: What do you enjoy doing (cooking, running, singing, writing, volunteering, working, mentoring, and so on)?

....

....

....

....

Roles: What roles do you have or have you held (teacher, administrator, parent, committee member, scout leader, coach, choir director)?

....

....

....

....

Experiences: What are some important experiences you have had (schools or universities; people known; locations visited, lived in, or hope to be visited)?

....

....

....

....

Find Common Ground

//

Who is someone with whom you want to find common ground?

....

....

....

....

Are you judging this person in any way that might make it difficult to find common ground?

....

....

....

....

What are some possible areas where common ground might exist or topics to avoid? Consider the acronym, ICARE.

....

....

....

....

I   *Interests such as books, food, music, sports teams, local restaurants ...*

C   *Convictions such as intellectual, political, religious ...*

A   *Activities such as cooking, running, singing, writing ...*

R   *Roles such as teachers, administrator, parent, committee member, scout leader, choir director ...*

E   *Experiences such as schools or universities attended, people known, locations visited or hoped to be visited ...*

What questions can you ask to find common ground?

....

....

....

....

CONTROL TOXIC EMOTIONS.

HABIT

///////////////.

8

Our destructive emotions can negatively affect us

in at least two ways: our emotions can keep us from

"I have decided to stick with love. Hate is too great a burden to bear."

///////////////,

MARTIN LUTHER KING, JR

saying something that should be said, or they can prompt us to say something

that we will regret. Either way, when we fail to control our emotions, we will

probably fail to have a better conversation. There are three simple strategies—

name it, reframe it, and tame it—we can use to keep our emotions under control.

Strategies to Redirect Toxic Emotions

1. Name It
2. Reframe It
3. Tame It

NAME IT

Triggers

Triggers are situations or words that make us feel a mix of deeply negative emotions, most often anger. Look back across the course of your life and see if you discover trigger patterns. Jot down a list of your common, personal triggers.

....

....

....

....

....

....

Root Cause

Now that you've listed a few of your common triggers, begin by picking one trigger and use The Five Whys (Root Cause Analysis) to identify the reason why you end up with this button being pushed. Don't feel you must limit yourself to only five whys. If you need more or fewer, that's fine. The main thing is to identify the root of your toxic emotions.

....

....

....

....

....

....

Action Plan

As the father referenced in the book finally understood the root cause of his anger, he was able to deal with his anger in a healthy, intentional way instead of just reacting. Given your own work through The Five Whys, how can you, also, begin to act with intention in the face of your trigger?

....

....

....

....

....

....

REFRAME IT

When you choose to reframe an emotionally difficult situation, you choose to adopt a growth mindset, which is a belief that you can change the way you react when others push your buttons. Reframing helps you change the way you think about emotionally difficult conversations by adopting a new frame for understanding them. There are four strategies you can use to help you accomplish this:

1. Think of Yourself as a Listener
2. Think of Yourself as a Learner
3. Have a Personal Victory
4. Go to the Balcony

At its essence, the concept of reframing is learning to use your mind to imagine the most positive spin possible on why things are happening. Perhaps the man referenced in the book was speeding through a stop sign because he was being irresponsible, but when you imagine his worry about his wife possibly being in labor, you are able to experience empathic distance that allows you to maintain a cool head where you normally would be tempted to react swiftly with a potent mix of negative emotions. The point isn't whether the man had a good reason to speed or not; the point is to trick your mind into an empathic type of response whereby you gain some much-needed control emotionally.

....
....
....
....
....
....

Think of Yourself as a Listener

Try thinking of yourself as being on a listening team and of others as being on a talking team. Your attentive listening will help your team earn more points and win the game. What other ways could you detach yourself from the conversation enough to be able to listen more objectively and rationally and less negatively? The main thing is to find a mental trick that hooks you into being a listener.

....
....
....
....
....

Think of Yourself as a Learner

Take the first tactic of being a listener a bit further, now. Your goal is to listen so closely that you're able to ask good questions and learn all you can about the other person and why he feels so badly. The point here is to let all the negative emotional fizz disperse in the wake of the greater adventure of learning all you can about the other person. One great thing about this strategy is that you will learn some amazing things about your partner.

....

....

....

....

....

....

Have a Personal Victory

Real personal power is taking responsibility for our own responses regardless of what the other person is bringing to the table. A conversation fraught with conflict may be infused with many personal victories—those times when, were there a keeper scoring controlled responses vs. reactionary emotional responses, the controlled responses team would be bringing in runner after runner across home plate. Every kind expression and every gentle tone is counted as a base hit that helps you win the game.

....

....

....

....

....

....

Go to the Balcony

To gain a calm, mental attitude of detachment is not a bad thing. It's as though you are a scientist, not emotionally attached to any particular theory, but always curious. Going to the balcony is a way to bring inner quietness and healthy emotional distance into a tough conversation.

....

....

....

....

....

....

TAME IT

Sometimes we don't have the luxury of time to prepare ourselves to emotionally handle negative conversations. We have to improvise on the fly, and the following four tactics can help:

1. Buy Time
2. Rewind the Tape
3. Break Vicious Cycles
4. Equilibrate the Conversation
5. Avoid Making Assumptions

BUY TIME TO THINK

Pause

Our moms and grandmothers told us to count to 10, and basically that was a simple way to remind ourselves to pause. There are many different ways to buy time to think in a tense negotiation. List a few ideas you have tried or could see yourself trying.

....

....

....

....

....

....

Timing

Consider the timing of your conversation and never make an important decision when you're flooded with emotion. What would some examples of bad timing look like?

....

....

....

....

....

REWIND THE TAPE

Check in with your partner by telling her everything you believe you've heard her say. That is, play the conversation back to her. Can you see yourself being able to do this? Does one or two of these strategies seem like a better fit for you than others? Consider why that might be.

....

....

....

....

....

....

BREAK VICIOUS CYCLES

Identify a type of situation where you nearly always get trapped into what Stone, Patton, Heen and Fisher call "what happened" conversations—conversations in which there are no winners. Like a merry-go-round that spins over and over the same old ground, it takes you nowhere, and it doesn't stop until somebody jumps off. How can you be that someone? What do you feel it would cost you to step out of that conversation? What would it look like to agree to disagree and move on?

....

....

....

....

....

....

....

AVOID ASSUMPTIONS

One of the hardest things to do is to suspend our assumptions. Like a scientist who tests theories, we should test our assumptions about others. As Ruiz points out, when you know what is true, you won't have any need for assumptions. What are some ways you can discover what is true about your conversation partner?

....

....

....

....

....

....

....

....

....

....

....

....

....

....

....

....

Control Toxic Emotions

What was the topic of the conversation?

....

....

....

Were you able to recognize that your hot buttons were going to be pushed?

○ Yes   ○ No

If no, what could you do differently in the future to recognize that what was happening was about to trigger an emotional response?

....

....

....

Were you able to reframe the conversation so that you could maintain control of your emotions?

○ Yes   ○ No

If yes, what did you do? If no, what could you do differently in the future to reframe the conversation and maintain control of your emotions?

....

....

....

What strategies did you use to maintain control of your emotions? Is there anything else you would like to try in the future?

....

....

What else could you try to do differently next time to maintain control of your emotions during difficult conversations?

....

....

....

....

Control Toxic Emotions
(1 of 2)

//.

ROOT CAUSE

Use this form to help you move through The Five Whys until you identify a root cause for your anger. Keep asking yourself why until you identify what needs to be changed, so you can extinguish your anger.

Briefly describe an experience that made you angry.

....

....

....

....

Why did that make you angry?

....

....

Why did that make you angry?

....

....

....

Why did that make you angry?

....

....

....

Why did that make you angry?

....

....

....

Why did that make you angry?

....

....

....

What is the root cause for your anger?

....

....

....

....

....

Control Toxic Emotions

(2 of 2)

MEDIA

Use this form to better understand how you physically react to prompts that make you feel strong, negative emotions. If you are a conservative, you might watch MSNBC. Pay attention to how your body reacts. By understanding your emotions, you'll be better able to prepare for situations that might previously have surprised you.

What did you notice about how your body reacted? Did your skin feel extra warm, heartbeat quicken, or breath feel short? Did you notice anything else about how your body reacted?

....

....

....

....

....

What did you notice about how you were feeling? Did you feel angry, frustrated, confused, helpless, overwhelmed, sad, or some other emotion?

....

....

....

....

....

....

What else did you notice about how you reacted to the prompt?

....

....

....

....

....

....

Control Toxic Emotions

///

Use this form to plan how you can use Name It, Reframe It, and Tame It strategies to plan on being in control during a conversation that has the potential to provoke you to react emotionally.

How will you recognize that your emotions are being provoked (skin feels extra warm, heartbeat quickens, shortness of breath, unclear thinking, desire to respond without thinking, or something else)?

....
....
....
....

How will you reframe the conversation, if necessary (seeing yourself as a listener, learner, game player, detached observer, or in some other way)?

....
....
....
....

How can you use empathy to better understand others' perspectives, in particular, their emotions and their needs?

....
....
....
....

What strategies can you use to tame your emotions to keep them under control (buy time, rewind the tape, break vicious cycles, equilibrate the conversation, avoid making assumptions, or something else)?

....
....
....
....

What else can you do to be prepared to control destructive emotions?

....
....
....
....

REFLECTIONS

REDIRECT TOXIC CONVERSATIONS.

9

Creating a setting where better conversations can flourish involves shaping the kind of conversations that happen around us. Kegan and Lahey (2001) say

"I have decided that there are too many people who enjoy hurting people with their words. I do not want to be in that camp."

//////////////.

ODESSA WARD

that a leader should be "a discourse-shaping language leader" (p. 20). That is, leaders must stand for a new kind of conversation while at the same time remaining a part of the school culture. We can create better conversations by never giving toxic conversations a chance to begin. Toxic conversations are ones in which people are diminished, considered inferior, or oppressed in some way. Thus, racist, sexist, and homophobic conversations are obviously toxic. Likewise, conversations that put people down or stereotype are also toxic. We do not promote a safe and healthy emotional environment by engaging in gossip, abuse, or blame. Fortunately, there are many ways in which we can shape conversations to avoid toxicity. We start by defining conversational norms and then learn and use effective strategies to redirect toxic conversations.

Defining Conversational Norms

It has been said by a number of communication theorists that what we communicate is what we build. We want to build a setting where safe, candid, respectful, open communication is the norm. In order to do this effectively, these norms should be established in partnership with team members. As an individual, what are the conversational norms you'd like to see prevail in your environment? In your classroom?

....

....

....

....

....

....

....

....

If you're working with team members, how can you create the psychological safety that may be needed to identify the types of conversation you'd like to consider as the norm for your building? Should you consider something like secret ballot voting for or against the proposed norms?

....

....

....

....

....

....

....

....

Consider how different it would feel to encourage and reinforce conversational norms that have been considered and accepted in a democratic format (as described above) vs. just saying, "We don't talk like that here."

....

....

....

....

....

....

....

....

As a person or team committed to continuous improvement, what might it look like to democratically revisit the conversational norms at regular intervals (every year or so)? List some ways this could be a good thing (e.g., new staff would have ownership of the norms and wouldn't feel like they were walking into a situation they have no understanding of or for which they have no ownership).

....

....

....

....

....

....

Imagine a building in which the highest conversational practices are the norm. What would it feel like to teach there? To collaborate? What would it feel like to be a student in this type of environment?

....

....

....

....

....

Strategies for Redirecting Toxic Conversation

You've identified what you'd like conversational norms to be in practice. However, you still have to deal with various forms of toxic conversations from time to time. To help you do that, here are a few strategies to reach for when the communication gets tough:

1. Define ToxicConversations
2. Identify Your Nonnegotiables
3. Stop Toxic Comments Before They Start
4. Use Responsive Turns
5. Silence

DEFINING TOXIC CONVERSATIONS (LEVEL 1 AND 2)

Level 1 comments are rarely spoken in public as they're obviously offensive. What are some examples of Level 1 toxic conversation topics?

....

....

....

....

....

....

Level 2 comments are ambiguous but destructive; for example, gossiping, blaming, and whining. What are some other types of Level Two comments?

....

....

....

....

....

....

....

IDENTIFY YOUR NONNEGOTIABLES: STOPPING TOXIC CONVERSATIONS BEFORE THEY START

The best way to do this is to democratically decide upon conversational norms—be they within your building, your Intensive Learning Team, your classroom, or (perhaps most powerfully), yourself. What are the things you will not speak? What are the conversations you will decide to redirect? (Revisit the previous section on creating conversational norms if necessary.)

....

....

....

....

....

....

....

....

USING RESPONSIVE TURNS TO REDIRECT TOXIC CONVERSATIONS

Strategies such as responsive turns enable us to focus on the words said instead of judging the person saying them.

Responsive Turn #1: Interrupting
What are some ways you can "stop the action" (Kolb & Williams) and allow yourself time to regroup when faced with a toxic conversation?

....

....

....

....

....

....

....

....

Responsive Turn #2: Naming

Tactful, yet pointed questioning (as opposed to questioning that is merely cloaked judgment) can help surface the truth and name behavior while still leaving room for the fact that people are at different points in their own growth. What types of questions can help name behavior while refraining from being judgmental?

....
....
....
....
....
....
....

Responsive Turn #3: Correcting

Correcting another adult is difficult. However, it helps to remember to focus on the words rather than the person (which defuses judgment and all the ill effects that go along with that). It is important to stop inaccurate information in its tracks, though, so what are some creative ways to provide corrective information without being a jerk? You cannot fight dehumanizing comments with dehumanizing corrections. How can you bring balance back to a conversation that is in need of it?

....
....
....
....
....
....
....

Responsive Turn #4: Diverting

Simply put, diverting is any way that you redirect a conversation away from a toxic topic. What are some creative ways by which you could effectively divert a toxic conversation?

....
....
....
....
....
....
....
....
....

Responsive Turns

Deborah Kolb and Judith Williams (2000) suggest that we can shape culture by redirecting conversations away from unhealthy topics, like gossip, by using communication maneuvers they call responsive turns. Responsive turns are communication tactics we can use to redirect potential unhealthy conversations. Four responsive turns suggested by Kolb and Williams, along with our definitions and some examples, are listed below.

TACTIC	WHAT IS IT?	EXAMPLE
Interupt	Cutting off the conversation before it begins	"Oh, darn. I'm late. I've gotta go."
Name	Describing what's going on so everyone can see it	"I just feel that if we keep complaining about kids, we're never going to come up with anything useful."
Correct	Clarify a statement that is not true	"I was at the meeting, and Mr. Smith was actually opposed to the plan."
Divert	Moving the conversation in another direction	"Speaking of Emily, is she still coaching tennis?"

REMAINING SILENT (STRATEGIC SILENCE)

In the book, *Strategic Silence* is referred to as a way to redirect toxic conversations. Sometimes one conversation partner feeds off of the response (good or bad) from the other. That is, as long as he has someone to talk to and who will respond to him in any way, he will continue his toxic conversation. To simply stop providing responses essentially cuts off the air for the speaker. In what other ways can silence be used strategically?

....

....

....

....

....

There are times when staying silent is an awful thing to do—"when good men do nothing ..." How is this silence different from strategic silence? How do you recognize when to use each type of silence? How can each type be effectively partnered with your conversational nonnegotiables?

....

....

....

....

....

....

....

....

....

....

....

....

....

....

....

....

....

....

....

....

....

....

....

....

LOOKING BACK:

Redirect Toxic Conversations

//

Use this form to look at a conversation where you either did or did not redirect a toxic conversation.

Briefly describe the conversation you experienced.

....

....

....

....

How quickly did you recognize that this was a conversation you needed to redirect?

....

....

....

....

What did you do to redirect the conversation (interrupt, name it, divert it, or some other method)?

....

....

....

....

Were you satisfied with the outcome of the conversation?

....

....

....

....

Is there anything you should do differently to be more effective next time you encounter a difficult conversation?

....

....

....

....

Redirect Toxic Conversations

How important is it for you to redirect toxic conversations?

....

....

....

....

How easy is it for you to redirect toxic conversations?

....

....

....

....

Do you remember a time when you failed to redirect a conversation that was toxic?

....

....

....

....

If so, what was the conversation about?

....

....

....

....

What can you do in the future to be better at redirecting toxic conversations?

....

....

....

....

Redirect Toxic Conversations

In the left-hand column below, list the kinds of conversations that you believe are never acceptable (racist, sexist, abusive, homophobic, gossiping, demeaning, blaming, or others).

Beside each topic, identify the strategy you will use to redirect the conversation (interrupt, name, correct, divert, or some other).

UNACCEPTABLE TOPICS	REDIRECTION STRATEGY

REFLECTIONS

BUILD TRUST.

10

"... Trust is one of the few variables that educational researchers have found that outstrips socioeconomic status as a predictor of student achievement."

///////////////.

MEGAN TSCHANNEN-MORAN

Many have written about the role of trust within professional learning. Amy Edmonson, the Novartis Professor of Leadership and Management at Harvard University, who has dedicated much of her academic life to studying how people work and learn together, concludes that people need to feel psychologically safe in order to be productive and learn. As Bryk and Schneider (2002) have written, trust is "forged in daily social exchanges—trust grows over time through exchanges where the expectations held for others are validated in action" (pp. 136–137).

CREDIBILITY X RELIABILITY X INTIMACY

SELF-FOCUS

Consider the statement, "When trust does not exist, there is caution, ... inertia, and fear." How does a lack of trust create each of those things? Think particularly about inertia. Often educators feel they're stuck within systems that are ... stuck. How does a lack of trust create this frustrating inertia?

....
....
....
....
....
....

"There is no greater source of distrust than advisors who appear to be more interested in themselves than in trying to be of service to clients" (Maister, Green, Galford). Consider the ways that selfishness and self-interest undermine each of the ingredients in trust.

The ingredients for trust are:
   » Character
   » Credibility
   » Reliability
   » Competence
   » Warmth
   » Stewardship

....
....
....
....
....
....
....
....
....
....
....
....

Character

» Do I have others' best interests at heart?
» Do I use hyperbole or exaggeration?
» Am I the kind of person who would lie to get something that I might not get if I were honest?
» At its root, flattery is a form of self-serving dishonesty. Reflect on how that is so.
» Do I gossip?
» Am I able to be humbly transparent even if it comes at the expense of looking good?

....
....
....
....

Reliability

UNDER-PROMISE AND OVER-DELIVER

In years past, it was said that a man's word was his bond. Reliability was a crucial part of being known as a trustworthy individual. While the adage has become almost cliché, reliability is still critical for building trust. How hard is it for you to be reliable? What stands in the way?

....
....
....
....
....

What would it look like for you to start under-promising and over-delivering?

....
....
....
....
....

How has a lack of reliability harmed school for students, teachers, and administration?

....
....
....
....
....

SAY NO

Saying no to something can be very difficult. Sometimes we are worried about what will happen (or not happen) when we remove ourselves from responsibility even though being able to focus on something we are better suited for is clearly the best option. What makes it hard for you to say no?

....
....
....
....
....
....
....

USE ORGANIZATIONAL RITUALS

What little routines can you add to your day to help you be more reliable?

....
....
....
....
....

Competence

SKILLS, KNOWLEDGE, & CREDIBILITY

Heidi Grant Halvorson talks about competence being the presence of three things: intelligence, skill, and effectiveness. Megan Tschannen-Moran writes about how it's not enough to merely have good intentions when it comes to being trustworthy. People need to know you have the stuff to back up your words. Like the coach referenced in the book did, consider your own intelligence, skill, and effectiveness. Which of those do you believe needs some shoring up?

....
....
....
....
....
....
....
....

Is competence more than merely having technical knowledge about something?

....
....
....
....
....
....

What are some ways to communicate competence without coming across as haughty?

....
....
....
....
....
....
....

To be competent is to be able to walk the talk, as the saying goes. How does this require humility?

....
....
....
....
....
....

Warmth

To show warmth is to listen, validate, demonstrate empathy, show positive attention, and be vulnerable.

Warmth is simply genuine kindness void of flattery while truly caring for another person. This can be clearly communicated by being a good listener. Do you agree with this statement?

....
....
....
....
....
....

Warmth is also demonstrated by validating others. How do you show the people in your circle of influence that you have faith in them? How do you show them the good you see in them (be a witness to the good)?

....
....
....
....
....
....

What can you do to show people you have empathy for them?

....
....
....
....
....

Why does judgment cut off any chance of intimacy (professional warmth and openness)?

....
....
....
....
....
....

Objectively, we must evaluate information about people. However, this is different from judging/condemning them. How can we take in information we need and make decisions without being judgmental, which is hurtful to the other person?

....
....
....
....
....
....

What would it look like for you to be emotionally honest—yet tactful—with others?

....
....
....
....

Stewardship

Think of one person you work with. What does it look like to put that person's interests ahead of your own?

There is flattery (self-serving dishonesty) and there is giving true credit to others for successes. What is the difference?

What are some specific ways you can choose service over self-interest? Push yourself to consider this in the context of a working relationship you struggle with.

If a large part of stewardship is a genuine focus on others, how can we display stewardship in conversation?

REFLECTIONS

Build Trust

///.

Who is someone that you really trust? What is it that makes them trustworthy?

....
....
....
....
....

Who is someone you do not trust? What is it that makes them untrustworthy?

....
....
....
....
....

Given what you've written above, is there anything you think you should do differently to be more trustworthy?

....
....
....
....
....

Building Trust

//

Use this form while watching a film or television program, or reading a novel, that has trustworthy and untrustworthy characters.

List all the ways the filmmaker or author depicts the trustworthy and untrustworthy characters:

TRUSTWORTHY	UNTRUSTWORTHY

Given what you noticed in the film, book, or program, is there anything you think you should do differently to be perceived as more trustworthy?

Building Trust

//

Use this form to consider the factors that influence trust—
character, competence, reliability, warmth, and stewardship.
Identify any changes you can make to become more trustworthy.

CHARACTER

Are you honest, transparent, and nonjudgmental? Do you need to
change so that you can be more trustworthy?

....

....

....

....

COMPETENCE

How can you increase the usefulness of what you share? Do you need
to be more focused or precise? Do you need to increase your depth of
knowledge?

....

....

....

....

RELIABILITY

What organizational rituals and boundaries can you add, or what
activities can you quit so you can be more reliable?

....

....

....

....

WARMTH

Do you need to get better at demonstrating empathy, listening,
being a witness to the good, or being vulnerable to encourage trust?

....

....

....

....

STEWARDSHIP

Do you need to change your outlook on life in any way so that you
are less concerned with yourself and more concerned with others?

....

....

....

....

REFLECTIONS

REFLECTIONS

A SAGE Company

Helping educators make the greatest impact

CORWIN HAS ONE MISSION: to enhance education through intentional professional learning.

We build long-term relationships with our authors, educators, clients, and associations who partner with us to develop and continuously improve the best evidence-based practices that establish and support lifelong learning.

Solutions you want. Experts you trust. Results you need.

AUTHOR CONSULTING

Author Consulting

On-site professional learning with sustainable results! Let us help you design a professional learning plan to meet the unique needs of your school or district. www.corwin.com/pd

INSTITUTES

Institutes

Corwin Institutes provide collaborative learning experiences that equip your team with tools and action plans ready for immediate implementation. www.corwin.com/institutes

eCOURSES

eCourses

Practical, flexible online professional learning designed to let you go at your own pace. www.corwin.com/ecourses

READ2EARN

Read2Earn

Did you know you can earn graduate credit for reading this book? Find out how: www.corwin.com/read2earn

Contact an account manager at (800) 831-6640 or visit **www.corwin.com** for more information.